M000159792

{Toddler*hood*

Scrapbooking Your Child's Early Years

From the Editors of
Memory Makers Books

Memory Makers Books
Cincinnati, Ohio

www.memorymakersmagazine.com

Toddlerhood. Copyright © 2007 by Memory Makers Books. Manufactured in the United States of America. All rights reserved. It is permissible for the purchaser to make the projects contained herein and sell them at fairs, bazaars and craft shows. No other part of this book may be reproduced in any form or by any electronic or mechanical means including information storage and retrieval systems without permission in writing from the publisher, except by a reviewer, who may quote a brief passage in review. Published by Memory Makers Books, an imprint of F+W Publications, Inc., 4700 East Galbraith Road, Cincinnati, Ohio 45236. (800) 289-0963. First edition.

11 10 09 08 07   5 4 3 2 1

Distributed in Canada by Fraser Direct
100 Armstrong Avenue
Georgetown, ON, Canada L7G 5S4
Tel: (905) 877-4411

Distributed in the U.K. and Europe by David & Charles
Brunel House, Newton Abbot, Devon, TQ12 4PU, England
Tel: (+44) 1626 323200, Fax: (+44) 1626 323319
E-mail: postmaster@davidandcharles.co.uk

Distributed in Australia by Capricorn Link
P.O. Box 704, S. Windsor, NSW 2756 Australia
Tel: (02) 4577-3555

Library of Congress Cataloging-in-Publication Data

Toddlerhood : scrapbooking your child's early years / from the editors of Memory Makers Books ; edited by Karen E. Davis.
    p. cm.
  Includes index.
  ISBN-13: 978-1-59963-007-6 (pbk.: alk. paper)
  ISBN-10: 1-59963-007-9 (pbk.: alk. paper)
1. Photograph albums. 2. Scrapbooks. 3. Photographs--Conservation and restoration. 4. Baby books. I. Davis, Karen E. II. Memory Makers Books.
TR501.T62 2007
745.593--dc22
                          2006100333

EDITOR: KAREN DAVIS
WRITER: HEATHER EADES
COVER DESIGNER: MARISSA BOWERS
DESIGNER: KARLA BAKER
ART COORDINATOR: EILEEN ABER
PRODUCTION COORDINATOR: MATT WAGNER
PHOTOGRAPHERS: TIM GRONDIN AND AL PARRISH
STYLIST: NORA MARTINI

contributing artists

Laura Achilles
Alecia Ackerman Grimm
Stephanie Barnard
Natalie Bensimhon
Leah Blanco Williams
Tonia Borrosch
Vicki Boutin
Phillipa Campbell
Erin Campbell-Pope
Samuel Cole
Marie Cox
Sheila Doherty
Tonya Doughty
Melanie Douthit
Amy Farnsworth
Kathy Fesmire
Valerie Fowler
Jennifer Gallacher
Maria Gallardo-Williams
Kelly Goree
Marie-Josee Guerin
Greta Hammond

Becky Heisler
Sandra Hicks
Nic Howard
Caro Huot
Kim Kesti
Sharon Laakkonen
Leana Lucas
Stacy McFadden
Kim Moreno
Barbara Pfeffer
Suzy Plantamura
Wendy Price
Leora Sanford
Rita Shimniok
Cindy Smith
Dana Swords
Shannon Taylor
Christine Traversa
Janine Wahl
Courtney Walsh
Amanda Williams
Beth Wolfgang

table of contents

toddler
MELT DOWN

LOVE

{Routine}
bed TIME

Remember the first time you went to the amusement park? You waited and waited for hours, it seemed, just to go for a spin on a three-minute ride of a lifetime. As a parent, thrills and chills come in the shape of a 2½-foot person, complete with the same speed, highs and lows of a roller coaster, which deliver that same indescribable feeling of intensified energy, controlled chaos and ultimate joy. This joyride is called Toddlerhood, a synchronized experience between your toddler and you. As your child discovers the wonders of the world, you rediscover them through fresh eyes and an untainted perspective.

Who better to shape this free-form personality than the community of loved ones embracing your child? With every hug from Grandma, your child's heart grows. With every life skill learned from Grandpa, your child's confidence grows. With each day spent with siblings and friends, your child develops compassion, caring, and the ability to laugh for the sake of being silly.

Keep track of these precious times of transformation. He may not remember the silly way he pronounced his sister's name at age three, but you will. Share the exhilaration of these years in scrapbook pages that will keep the thrill of this amazing ride at the forefront of your heart, when you're back in the station waiting to blast off into the next miraculous stage of your child's life.

chapter **one**
growing
& learning

It happens so fast. One day we snuggle our tiny, helpless newborn into her crib, while she does little but take in her new surroundings, cry a little when discomforted, and wrap us around her little finger. The next day, we go to pick up our 7-pound miracle and are shocked to retrieve 30 pounds of huggable, non-stop energy—attitude and all! When did this happen?! And it only speeds up from there. Cherish these times of fascination and fun, as you see and discover the world once again from the perspective of your child. Experience the power and artistry in nature as your child takes in the majesty of a rainfall. Encourage and applaud your child's efforts as he tackles the tasks of life we take for granted— dressing himself, learning to spit toothpaste and moving the pedals on that first tricycle. Celebrate each stage of your child's development through meaningful layouts and projects that will be treasured by both you and your child as you look back in the years ahead to see just how far you both have come.

Explore your world.

TA DA!

Sing and dance just because.

Look at everyday as a gift.

Be silly.

Be amazed at the little things.

Enjoy this gift of life.

explore your world

Marie Cox
Raleigh, North Carolina

Get down on your hands and knees to gather great perspectives of your child's world as he or she explores it. Marie captured her child's determination in putting objects together on this colorful creation, and added her own sage advice to her child in journaling strips below. Buttons are always a simple means to lend bursts of color and a childlike quality to your page, and as Marie shows here, a festive way to give dimension and repetition to polka dot patterns.

supplies: Patterned paper (Chatterbox); sticker (7 Gypsies); buttons (unknown); cardstock

Kelly Goree
Shelbyville, Kentucky

The inspiration evoked from a child's imagination can come alive in your own page designs to cherish their stages of creativity. Be it fingerpaints, a new box of crayons, or Play Doh, the bright colors and bright ideas your child comes up with in his artistic experiences make for playful and powerful layouts. Choose vibrant and varying patterns in ribbons and papers to capture the excitement. Your title can be a dynamic dimensional element by following Kelly's example, covering two sizes of chipboard squares with cardstock, rounding the corners, sanding and inking them for definition. Adhere chipboard letters on top of two stacked chips.

supplies: Patterned paper, rub-ons, sticker (KI Memories); chipboard squares (Bazzill); chipboard letters (Heidi Swapp); rickrack (Doodlebug); ribbon (Offray); pigment ink; pen; cardstock

urban jedi

Barbara Pfeffer
Omaha, Nebraska

Pull all the motion and energy of your child onto your page designs through chipboard arrows, as Barbara models on this vibrant and fast-paced layout. By using a black pen to create squiggly lines around her arrows, broken with brad dots for visual interest, she furthers the feel of excitement and motion, while pulling the viewer's eye around the different page elements. Cohesiveness is created by using the same squiggly, broken pen lines around letter stickers in the title and inside the patterned paper and journaling strips.

supplies: Patterned paper (Junkitz); chipboard details (Heidi Swapp, Li'l Davis); letter stickers (SEI); brads; pen; cardstock; TXT Stonewashed font (Inspire Graphics)

endless possibilities

Erin Campbell-Pope

Petal, Minnesota

The sky's the limit when it comes to your toddler's playtime occupations, and an adorable mini album like this one is a great place to store images of your child at play, trying on different careers for size. Erin found that the mini album saved both time and space and makes for a charming keepsake. To make your own mini album, keep it simple, using the same sketch for each layout and a unified color scheme throughout. To eliminate bulk and further the simplicity, paper pieced mini embellishments keep style big and stress to a minimum.

supplies: Patterned paper (My Mind's Eye, Paper Studio); letter stickers (Doodlebug, Mrs. Grossman's); brads (Chatterbox, Queen & Co.); flowers (Prima, Queen & Co.); jewelry tag (Making Memories); chipboard oval (Fancy Pants); twill ribbon (unknown); embellishments (EK Success, Sandylion); decorative scissors; circle punch; dye ink; cardstock

first and last swimming lesson

Tonya Doughty

Wenatchee, Washington

Some of your children's first experiences may also be their last at a particular age. A single shot of an activity tried is still a memory worth preserving and deserves a page of its own. Fold an envelope back behind itself at an angle to create a visually appealing and multi-purpose page element. Tuck the details of the event inside the envelope for safe keeping. A simple and playful way to spice up the look of a typed journaling block is to leave intermittent blanks to fill in with handwritten words. Carry the look onto the rest of the page, as Tonya demonstrates here, by combining handwriting into the name and age categories created with rubber stamps.

supplies: Patterned paper (Die Cuts With A View, My Mind's Eye, ANW Crestwood); envelope (Waste Not Paper); letter stamps (EK Success); name and date stamps (Jenni Bowlin); pigment ink; acrylic tiles, rub-on (KI Memories); ribbon (Offray); pen; cardstock

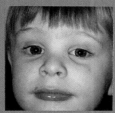

not a **problem**

I love my son, Lucas. But he has not been the easiest child to raise. From the moment he was born, he has had a scream that could curdle milk... and he used it. He's strong-willed, easily frustrated and hard to manage. Because of that, he is a challenge, what some might term " a problem child."

As his mother, I refuse to see him that way. I may not know how to deal with him sometimes, but I will never stop trying. I admit there have been a few times when I have completely lost my temper with him & yelled when I should have taken a deep breath. Okay, more than a few. For that I am sorry and pray that he forgives me my imperfections as a mom. Honestly, it breaks my heart to think that I may have broken his.

And there are moments with him each day where I think that all the negative things, they couldn't exist because the moment is so perfect. He comes to me out of the blue and gives me a hug and an "I love you, Mommy." Moments where he selflessly shares with his sister. Moments that touch my heart and make me realize what a sweet spirit he has.

Some nights when I go into his room to check on him, I watch him sleep and my heart just breaks. I feel such a heaviness. I so want to get through to him. I want to help heal the part of himself that makes him get so frustrated, so hard to be with. But even as his mom, there are things about him that I can't change. I can guide him and pray for him, but he is the way he is.

I love him and see what a special little boy he is. At just four years old, he has such a creative & imaginative mind. He is sweet and smart and silly.

That has to be one of the toughest parts about being a parent. It's one of things that the parenting books don't prepare you for. Some kids are more challenging to raise than others. And sometimes it's not something you can just fix. As much as you would like to, you can't live your child's life or make their choices for them. Even at just four years old.

But you know what the amazing thing is? You love them anyway. I love Lucas. For his sweetness and creativity, but also for his stubbornness and difficulties. They are all a part of the complete package that make up my wonderful son. They are how God designed him to be.

I'll wait him out. I know that some of the things that he struggles with will improve with age. Some of them will still be there. Even though I sometimes get frustrated with him that it doesn't mean that I don't love him. Maybe that's where he gets it from? But I want him to know that no matter what he does, I'll keep loving him. That's definitely not a problem.

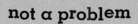

not a problem

Sheila Doherty

Coeur d'Alene, Idaho

While some children seem easier to raise than others, they are all unique individuals with personalities that beam through on pages like the one Sheila created about her son. This two-page spread sets the stage for a border of photos on the left, stepping through a sequence of the difficult moments of child-raising to the beaming face in a single photo on the right that makes parenthood so worth the effort. Heartfelt journaling gives a mother's reflections on a challenging child's struggles on the left, while the right focuses on his strengths. Rounded photo edges, with a revolving title wrapped around, emphasize the child's moment to shine.

supplies: Patterned paper (Flair Designs); circle letters (Making Memories); rub-on (Creative Imaginations); ribbon (SEI); corner rounder; cardstock

Kim Kesti
Phoenix, Arizona

The many passions of your toddler, from dinosaurs to Dora, make for layouts sure to be treasured long after the trains and tricycles have been tucked away. Catch your child in action with that special blanket, or ferocious T-Rex, as Kim's son shows here. Create the look of an identification card, as Kim did, utilizing one close-up image and vital statistics surrounding your child's favorite pastime. Punched paper squares and circles provide a primary feel, while a paperclip accent lends formality and fun.

supplies: Patterned paper, decorative stickers (Provo Craft); chipboard letters (Heidi Swapp); journaling tag (7 Gypsies); paper clip (Target); brad; word accents (Making Memories); adhesive foam; pen; cardstock

rescuing a lizard

Jennifer Gallacher
American Fork, Utah

The first time you witness your child exhibiting values close to any family's heart, such as kindness and compassion for others, you want to have a camera nearby! A large close-up image of your child in the act of learning a treasured trait, as Jennifer shows on this layout of her son saving the life of a lizard, will preserve the memory of this monumental moment. Use papers and accents to play up the value demonstrated, as Jennifer did here using graph paper with a hand stitched heartbeat line and a large chipboard heart beside the title to emphasize the sanctity-of-life theme of her page.

supplies: Patterned paper (BasicGrey, Deja Views, Karen Foster, KI Memories, Sandylion, Scenic Route); die-cut letters (Deja Views); letter stamps (Li'l Davis); acrylic paint; chipboard heart (Heidi Swapp); large brads (Karen Foster); circle punch; date stamp; embroidery floss; photo corner; stamping ink; cardstock; You've Got Mail font (Scrapsupply)

make art

Kim Kesti

Phoenix, Arizona

The rapid speed of toddlerhood is enough to make any parent have to catch their breath! Even though Kim's photos were taken only three years ago, the changes between ages one and three are astounding! While it's always fun to scrap as your child grows, sometimes saving sentimental images for a few years allows for more reflective journaling, as you are then able to stand back in awe of the many changes that have occurred in your child. Fill a single page with several images of your child in the midst of one of his or her favorite pastimes and then note the changes and similarities in the details between then and now, such as chubby hands, favorite first haircuts and other telltale signs from the photos.

supplies: Patterned paper, number stickers (KI Memories); ledger paper (Making Memories); letter stickers (American Crafts, KI Memories); word sticker (Scrapworks); rub-ons (Autumn Leaves); corner rounder; dye ink; pen; cardstock

Tonia Borrosch
Honeaye Falls, New York

When the tooth fairy makes her first visit to your child, take proper care in brushing up on your journaling skills to record the details of this momentous occasion, as Tonia did here on this timeless treasure. A single black-and-white close-up shot will help you remember the first of many-to-come smiles with holes, while serving as the focus of the page. Strips of text printed along the side are a non-obtrusive means to record the date the first tooth was lost, events surrounding the loss, and of course the monetary amount the tooth fairy donated! A dominant title along the top balances out a strip of patterned paper along the bottom, while keeping the eye centered on the subject.

supplies: Patterned paper, letter stickers, rub-ons (Arctic Frog); brads; dye ink; cardstock; Times New Roman font (Microsoft)

tooth fairy tin

Kathy Fesmire
Athens, Tennessee

Losing a tooth is cause for great celebration when it involves a special delivery to the tooth fairy in a magical tin. Kathy altered her Altoid tin with inked paper, decoupaging the chipboard letters and letter stickers into a message for the highly anticipated fairy. A glitter-enhanced wand, with delicate star accents flowing from a sheer ribbon tie adds to the magic. A patterned-paper envelope embellished with more celestial accents fits neatly inside the treasured tin, providing the perfect place to exchange a tooth for the going rate. These tins fit neatly on a dresser or nightstand, rather than under a pillow, allowing easy access for the tooth fairy, while minimizing chances of disturbing a sleeping child.

supplies: Candy tin; patterned paper (My Mind's Eye); letter stickers (EK Success); chipboard letter (Li'l Davis); star charms (Crafts Etc.); ribbon (Offray); wooden star (Plaid); acrylic paint; dye ink; decoupage medium; glitter

no more tooth

Kelly Goree
Shelbyville, Kentucky

An actual memento of a lost first tooth makes for an endearing and visually intriguing element when attached to a page. A transparency pocket can be handmade to hold the treasured tooth, stapled closed and then tucked into a metal label holder adhered to your design. Use several images to showcase different angles and expressions to remember the event. Kelly used a small sheet of notebook paper to play up the childhood nostalgia of the page.

supplies: Patterned paper, chipboard shapes, letter sticker (BasicGrey); chipboard letters, plastic letters, rub-ons (Heidi Swapp); bookplate (Making Memories); stickers (7 Gypsies); stamps (Fontwerks); dye ink; thread; notebook paper; pen; cardstock

twos

Barbara Pfeffer

Omaha, Nebraska

The clever and unique ways your child learns to do something, such as hold a pencil, try to whistle or show their age, are a large portion of the toddlerhood fun. Savor these moments on a graphic-looking spread, using a large photo of your child in action to fill the bulk of the left-hand page. A patterned paper strip composed of simple shapes creates an energizing border when set beside it. Create a unifying flow between pages, overlapping the left-hand image with a matted accent photo. Allow the negative space on the page to create its own design on the right by spacing out your title, subtitle and journaling blocks.

supplies: Patterned paper (KI Memories); letter stickers (Chatterbox); photo turns (Junkitz); brads; cardstock; LD Tall Pen font (Inspire Graphics)

me too

Little Miss nearly-two. Braden's birthday party.

The back yard is full of boys and noise. Big boys games. | Not the most suitable place for a toddler.

You ran around with the boys as much as you could. | You were so involved that you refused to sleep.

Although being the youngest has its advantages. | There are times when it has its disadvantages as well.

If I could make a bet on what you were thinking in this photo, | I would bet you were thinking "me too?"

Nic Howard

Pukekohe, New Zealand

When younger siblings feel left in the shadows of an older brother or sis, help your big-kid-wannabes shine like the stars they truly are with a page of their very own, like Nic created here. A dynamic single photo pulls full attention onto your little one, while hooks added to the photo edges provide security for coordinating cord to wrap your loved one's image in a textural hug. A large circle in the background puts your child in the spotlight, while shimmering, shiny embellishments, including bead trim, silver snaps and sequin trim, enhance the effect.

supplies: Patterned paper (Junkitz); chipboard letters (Making Memories, Pressed Petals); acrylic paint; cord and beaded trims, notions (unknown); corner rounder; dye ink; decoupage medium; photo preserver (Krylon); pen; cardstock

Jake's Jargon

Mom often has a chuckle listening to words that are crisp and clear as a bell. Hearing them said by her little boy is often the cutest thing in the world. Other times, when you spit out a word, that Mom swears is your own secret language. They are curious words, often filled with strange sounds that are not of the English alphabet. Throaty gurgles that form nothing remotely close to a word, mean something important to Jake. Mom is not always sure what you want, and sometimes you *think* you need that thing right away, but most times you are just content to talk Mom's ear off about everything and nothing at the same time. And it doesn't matter that she can only figure out one word in five, you manage to hold her attention with your cute little jargon.

Elephant pronounced: (el' pant) Positively your favorite animal.

Yogurt pronounced: (doh' dur) Favorite snack. Could eat gallons.

Blanket pronounced: (Baa' deh) Can't go to bed without it.

jake's jargon

Janine Wahl
Sylvan Lake, Alberta, Canada

When your child learns to talk your talk, parents must kick up their own learning instincts a notch to translate your child's new "foreign" language. Janine designed this charming layout to remember the adorable ways her son pronounced each of his new words, and the journey she had as a parent in deciphering the meanings behind each customized sound he made. A cut wavy stripe from a free-flowing patterned paper provides a colorful, childlike element and cheery contrast against the vast dark background. Janine used photos along her right-hand border to illustrate each of her child's favorite vocabulary words, with pronunciation cues set beside them.

supplies: Patterned paper (Urban Lily); circle punch; dye ink; cardstock; Arbuckle Remix font, Avant Garde BKBT font (Internet download)

green

Tonia Borrosch
Honeoye Falls, New York

There will be many stages and phases that will be dear to your heart long after toddlerhood is over. Savor those memories, such as developments in speech and colors, on a page design that celebrates the unique and fun daily experiences you share with your child. To keep a page focused on your journaling, incorporate a typical conversation between yourself and toddler into your text, adding only a single photo of your child at the time of the documented phase—a simple and fun way to keep the small stuff big in your memory.

supplies: Patterned paper (Karen Foster); handmade paper (unknown); square punch; cardstock; 2 Peas Evergreen font (Two Peas in a Bucket); Dirty Ego, Jump Start fonts (Dafont)

It's ALL about

GREEN.

You are now 28 months old and you are starting to become familiar with your colors. It appears as if you have an immediate favorite-that being green. I think it is truly the only color you can correctly match up at least 90% of the time. You are getting pretty good with yellow and orange too, but that green still seems to be stuck right in the front of that memory bank. Here is a typical conversation we have at least once a day:

Mommy: Ethan, what color is the froggy?
Ethan: GREEN
Mommy: Very good Ethan! What color is the ducky?
Ethan: GREEN
Mommy: Try again.
Ethan: YELLOW
Mommy: Very good!
Mommy: What is your name?
Ethan: Efin
Mommy: How old are you?
Ethan: GREEN
Mommy: No Ethan, I said how old are you?
Ethan: GREEN
Mommy: No Ethan, you are two years old.
Mommy: What color is Savannah (our yellow lab)?
Ethan: GREEN

We are working on colors daily and read Brown Bear each night before bed. It just makes me smile when I know that you are going to say GREEN when I ask you just about ANY question! I will be a little sad when this cute little phase passes, because right now that is part of what makes you who you are at 28 months old.

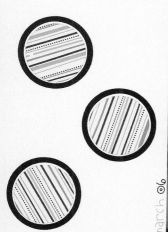

'I*C*K'

"That spells Nick"

march '06

Don't think your sisters aren't getting an awful lot of mileage out of this one, buddy!

ick, that spells nick

Barbara Pfeffer
Omaha, Nebraska

A simple yet dynamic title is sometimes all it takes to remember a funny family incident, as Barbara shows on this page commemorating her son's first attempts to spell his name. A single photo with a lot of personality can perfectly illustrate a humorous quote from your child, with simple accents, such as patterned paper circles and coordinating ribbon, balancing the look with texture and whimsy. Colorful brads used to balance out opposing corners at the top and bottom of your page lend dimension and repeat the look of circular accents added for movement.

supplies: Patterned paper, letter stickers, rub-ons (Doodlebug); chipboard details (Heidi Swapp); ribbon (Maya Road); brads; die-cut shapes (Sizzix); cardstock; My Own Topher font (Internet download)

words tag book

Amy Farnsworth
Brighton, Colorado

Your child develops a vocabulary so quickly, it can seem a daunting task to keep up with those baby book entries! Amy enjoyed the freedom this simple tag book allowed her, providing an easy-to-adjust means for recording her daughter's new words in a monthly format. A basic metal ring is all that is needed to begin adding tags to your own developmental design. Use these tag albums as stand-alone memory pieces, or incorporate them into a larger format baby album.

supplies: Patterned paper, rub-ons, stickers, tags (Three Bugs in a Rug); letter stickers (American Crafts, Creative Imaginations, Doodlebug, KI Memories, Li'l Davis); ribbon (Li'l Davis, May Arts); buttons (Autumn Leaves); clear heart (Heidi Swapp); embroidery floss; silk flowers (craft supply store); metal ring (Avery); pen; cardstock; Blink, Long & Lean, Katrina Style and Zing fonts (In a Blink of an Eye)

daddy (dadeee) cracker (cah cah)

mommy bridey (brh nee) banana (nana)

left foot right

Amy Farnsworth
Brighton, Colorado

The daily life happenings that grown-ups take for granted, such as buttoning a coat, learning to spit toothpaste, or getting those shoes on the correct feet, are an everyday battle for a developing toddler. Layouts, such as Amy's page design, remind us to not sweat the small stuff and help us view life through our children's eyes. Amy snapped this image of her son when he had a frustrated look on his face, capturing this stage of battling his appropriate shoe sides. A slightly staggered title can balance out a page with a single image at the top, providing a unique and dynamic element on its own. Dominantly blue patterned papers and ink smudges help create an all-boy look on the page.

supplies: Patterned paper (Chatterbox); letter stickers (Junkitz, Mustard Moon); chipboard letters (Heidi Swapp); chipboard accents (Li'l Davis); brads; photo turns (unknown); thread; yarn; dye ink; cardstock; Stop Sign font (Two Peas in a Bucket)

love you

Tonia Borrosch
Honeoye Falls, New York

The first time your child says, "I love you," is an imprint that never leaves a mother's heart, as Tonia shows here on this layout celebrating her son's first attempts to sign the phrase. Keep the page simple and focused on the child's attempts, be it through a hug, blowing a kiss or other means, and let your journaling share the details. By staggering journaling strips into two balanced sections on the page, you can create playful arrangements overtop complementary patterned papers, which need only an embellishment or two, such as the thematic Scrabble letter box, as Tonia added here.

supplies: Patterned paper (Colorbök, KI Memories); ribbon (Offray); brads; wooden letters (EK Success); cardboard circle pouch (unknown); dye ink; pigment ink; cardstock; Dirty Ego font (Dafont)

amazing imagination

Maria Gallardo-Williams
Cary, North Carolina

Everyday items such as boxes, shoes or an old tennis ball, as Maria captures on this layout, serve as a launching point for your child's imagination. Catch the wonder of your child's innovative spirit in playful images that will enhance the pages of his toddler years scrapbooks. Filling your page with several images that display the many ways your toddler uses a single item is sure to inspire and spark your own imagination. Maria balanced her photo-packed page by adding a title block in the upper left, with an embellished first letter created with simple die-cuts.

supplies: Patterned paper (Karen Foster); die-cut letters, twill (Legacy Paper); rub-ons (Scrapworks); dye ink; cardstock

potty reward jar

Kathy Fesmire
Athens, Tennessee

Potty training can mean big fun for your toddler with an eye-catching Reward Jar. A mini glass milk bottle serves as the starting point for these creations, which can be tailored to win the affection of either boys or girls. Ribbons, torn denim strips and leather threads can be added to please the cowboy in your household, with a mini bandana, rope and a sheriff's badge completing the look. For girly-girl appeal, cover a chipboard tag with a sweet, sassy print and embellish with a pink flower accent. Fill your jars with candy, stickers or other special treats that will get your little one out of diapers in record time!

supplies: Glass milk bottle (Hobby Lobby); patterned paper (Paper Studio); rub-on letters, circle punch (EK Success); ribbons (American Crafts, Offray); buttons, chipboard, flower (unknown); dye ink; decoupage medium; cardstock

crooked funny smile

Phillipa Campbell
Jerrabomberra, Australia

It's not only our children's cuteness but their quirks as well that endear them to our hearts. Be sure to capture your child's silly expressions and hilarious habits on their own pages, as Phillipa shows with her son's "camera face." You can energize pages with simplistic photos by pulling out the colors from the images into more intricate backgrounds. Phillipa balanced the comical subject matter of her page by contrasting the theme with a more formal look in her patterned papers and covered slide frames, while embellishing with whimsical buttons and an offset title.

supplies: Patterned paper (7 Gypsies, BasicGrey, Chatterbox); chipboard letters (Heidi Swapp); buttons (Chatterbox, SEI); ribbon (American Crafts); frames (unknown); thread; decorative scissors; pen

STELL'S NEW BIG girL Bug gy bEdROOm

"out" with your crib + "in" with the bugs.

I took Stella to Ikea for a big girl mattress + came home with bug print bedding, wall lamps, curtains (which aren't hung yet in these photos) + a huge rainbow bed canopy. who knew that she loves cute little bugs!?

snail

dragonfly

lady bug

butterfly

dragonfly

We set up the room that afternoon + she has slept in there by herself everyday since. way to go Stella! —mom '05

buggy bedroom

Alecia Ackerman Grimm

Atlanta, Georgia

After the crib has been tucked snuggly away into storage, create a layout to celebrate your child's new big-kid bedroom. Play up the dominant colors from the room, as Alecia did with her daughter's rainbow bed canopy, pulling them into the background with strips of vibrant colored papers. Employ coordinating colors into the title through a variety of letter stickers and rub-ons. Thematic stickers, such as these cute little bugs, are a simple way to highlight the theme of a room, with corresponding labels interspersed between the arrangement. To establish an informal, comfy bedroom feel, handwritten journaling in a free-flowing journaling block sets the tone.

supplies: Patterned paper, bug stickers (Scissor Sisters); letter stickers (Making Memories); rub-on accents (Doodlebug, KI Memories); photo corners (Heidi Swapp); pen; cardstock

SAY GOODBYE TO YOUR CRIB

SUGAR & SPICE & EVERYTHING NICE

You said "goodbye" to your crib on November 17, 2005 at the age of 21 months. Not only could you climb in and out of your crib, you liked to jump up and down holding on to the bars - and it was very scary that you could jump as high as you did. It was time to go to a big-girl bed. We told you this was your last time in your baby bed, and while you were at school the next day, daddy packed up your crib.

goodbye crib

Melanie Douthit
West Monroe, Louisiana

Climbing out, jumping too high and monkey-like acrobatics are just a few of the signals parents get when their child is ready to move out of the crib. Melanie designed a fun and feminine farewell salute to her daughter's crib. Capturing her daughter in action illustrates her readiness for a big-girl bed. Rub-ons provide a simple way to lend the look of hand-stitching to a page, without all the hassle. Hand cut elements from patterned paper and arrange in playful compositions about your page.

supplies: Patterned paper (Paper Salon); rub-ons, stickers (Flair Designs); chipboard accent (Everlasting Keepsakes); acrylic paint; cardstock; Tekton Pro font (Internet download)

big girl room

Sandra Hicks
San Antonio, Texas

The transition to a big-kid bed is an emotional experience for the whole family. Cherish your child's emotions as she embraces her new and improved bedroom through photos that capture the feelings expressed, and images that showcase the new bedroom décor. A simple and sweet journaling block can capture mom's emotions and the difficulty of packing up a crib and the memories that came along with it. Patterned papers reflective of the room's look and feel can be layered for an endearing background, while coordinating rickrack pulls the viewer's eye around the layout. Buttons and machine stitching soften the layout's look and lend homespun charm.

supplies: Patterned paper (BasicGrey, Chatterbox, Memories Complete); title letters (Heidi Swapp); chipboard flowers (Maya Road); rub-ons (Chatterbox); brad; buttons (Autumn Leaves); rickrack (Karen Foster); thread; cardstock; Arial Narrow font (Microsoft)

BIG girl ROOM

Well the day finally came for you to get a big girl bed. No more crib. I admit that I did shed a tear at the thought of no longer being able to pick up my little baby out of the crib or set you in there each night. So many memories - it is hard to let it go. As much as it is exciting to see you do new things and grow up, it is also a little sad for me too. So we bought your new bed, dresser and nightstand, and you love it! You have done so well in your big girl bed. You usually go right to sleep after I read a few of your books. Once in awhile you'll get back up, but I think you just like having me tuck you back in! ☺ ☺ Mommy

It only took a couple of weeks this spring. Everyday we would push you up and down the street on your bike, making the pedals turn so you could feel how it worked. Within no time, you were turning the pedals yourself. At first you were very cautious, making sure not to go too fast, but now you are an old pro, frantically pedaling to catch up with the big kids. Such a fun step in your growth and development.

learning to ride

Greta Hammond
Goshen, Indiana

Your creative wheels are sure to start spinning when designing a layout to record your child's first "big-kid bike" experience. A large patterned-paper circle serves as a dynamic backdrop. With the look of a tire, the circle is perfect for arranging your photos overtop, keeping their edges straight for contrast. Greta furthered the round wheel effect by adding circular accents in coordinating colors along with pretty, pink brads. The sharp angles of super star embellishments balance the circle-style look of the layout with edginess and fun.

supplies: Patterned paper, coaster letters and shapes (Imagination Project); fabric letters (Scrapworks); brads; pen; cardstock

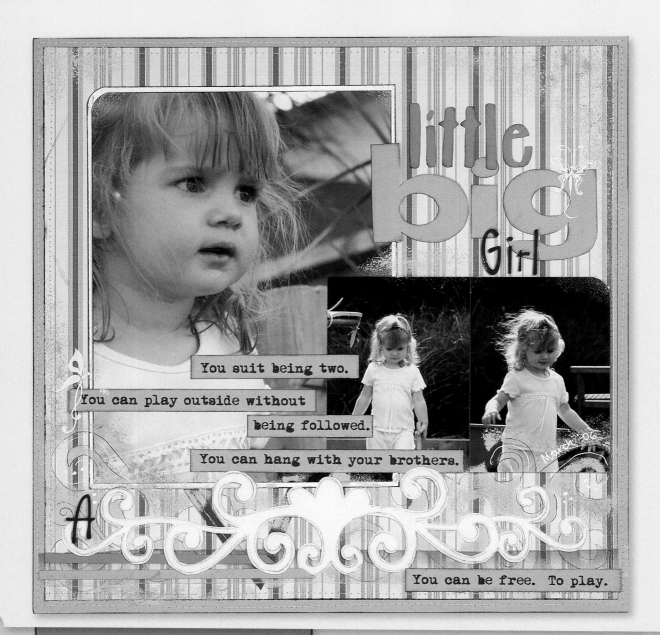

little big girl

Nic Howard

Pukekone, New Zealand

While special events are always page worthy, don't forget to record the quiet moments of every-day life to celebrate your child's growth and development. Nic took long-distance, candid shots of her daughter to capture natural poses of her two-year old. A hand-cut, velvety design at the bottom of the page serves as a bold and beautiful element on its own, and can be used to sponge paint overtop photos and background for a softened, whisper-soft feel.

supplies: Patterned paper (Chatterbox); rub-ons (BasicGrey); velvet (SEI); acrylic paint; solvent ink; corner rounder; thread; ribbons (unknown); cardstock; Airplane font (Two Peas in a Bucket); Mom's Typewriter font (Dafont)

growth chart

Amanda Williams
Tucson, Arizona

Your child is growing fast, so keep tabs on the details through a photo growth chart, visually showcasing your baby's physical leaps and bounds. Be sure to leave several spaces for multiple photos within each year of your toddler's growth, as a matter of months can mean a multitude of inches during growth spurts. Black-and-white photos create a cohesive look against a festive background, which can be tailored to suit either a little boy or girl. Amanda decoupaged her patterned paper, a plastic tape measure and playful accents to a 5-foot wooden board, which she will hang 9 inches from the ground. The theme of flowers re-emphasizes the topic of blossoming and growing.

supplies: Wood board; patterned paper (Urban Lily); fabric flowers, plastic letters (Heidi Swapp); die-cut sunflower (Colorbök); circle punch; plastic tape measure; dye ink; decoupage medium; cardstock

growing up

Marie-Josee Guerin
Pointe-aux Trembles, Quebec, Canada

Capturing the emotion of a milestone moment, such as standing for the first time on tip-toes to do something independently, can be further enhanced through up-close images of the details. Keep the photos black-and-white to emphasize the event, and use colors and patterns in the background that play up the memory. Create a unique embellishment by allowing numbers on measuring tape twill to peak through a painted chipboard shape. Add a concho to highlight your child's age.

supplies: Patterned paper, die-cut letters (Daisy D's); letter stickers (Doodlebug); chipboard accents (Fancy Pants, Heidi Swapp); photo turns (Junkitz); brads; rub-ons (Heidi Swapp, Melissa Frances); concho (Scrapworks); pigment ink; circle punch; thread; cardstock; Grace font (Internet download)

29

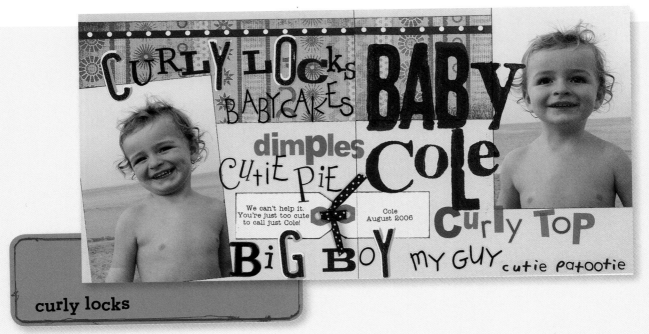

curly locks

Dana Swords
Doswell, Virginia

The precious nicknames that accompany your toddler along his journey to childhood are great items to record in a scrapbook celebrating this age. Use a couple of images that capture the essence of his or her nicknames, as Dana demonstrates here on this two-page spread. A variety of letter stickers and/or rub-on letters and letter stamps can be intertwined to make a visually stimulating page design made up simply of your child's pet names. A patterned paper border along the top gives a two-page spread colorful energy and flow.

supplies: Patterned paper (BasicGrey, Chatterbox); letter stickers (Deluxe Designs, K&Co., Miss Elizabeth's, Provo Craft, Sticker Studio); chipboard letters (Heidi Swapp); rub-ons (Miss Elizabeth's); tags (unknown); ribbon (Offray); foam stamps (Li'l Davis, Magnetic Poetry, Making Memories); acrylic paint; dye ink; cardstock; Teletype font (Internet download)

becoming a real boy

Barbara Pfeffer
Omaha, Nebraska

For any parent of girls, having a baby boy is a whole new ballgame, as Barbara's journaling attests. Celebrate the differences in gender as your baby becomes a full-fledged little boy on a rough and tumble layout such as this one. For a simple background, choose patterned papers with a grunge-effect edge or use sandpaper for distressing papers and elements yourself. A complementary blue and orange color scheme are perfect for establishing a masculine look on your page with an energetic and joyful kick.

supplies: Patterned paper, brads, letter buttons, photo turns, rub-ons (Junkitz); clear buttons (7 Gypsies); embroidery floss; craft punch; cardstock; AL Featherbrained font (Two Peas in a Bucket)

LOOKING AT THESE PICTURES I TOOK OF YOU AT THE PARK, I SUDDENLY REALIZED HOW BIG YOU ARE. OVER THE LAST YEAR, YOU HAVE GROWN IN HEIGHT TREMENDOUSLY, BUT IT'S MORE THAN JUST THAT. YOUR PERSONALITY HAS BLOSSOMED INTO A HAPPY, SWEET AND FUNNY LITTLE GIRL. TODAY AT THE PLAYGROUND, YOU DIDN'T NEED MY HELP TO CLIMB. NOW WHEN WE ARE WALKING, YOU ARE TOO BIG TO HOLD MY HAND. YOU DON'T NEED CARRIED ANYMORE AND ARE TOO BIG FOR ME TO CRADLE IN MY ARMS LIKE I USED TO. YOU ARE MAKING YOUR OWN DECISIONS AND I WANT YOU TO REMEMBER, NO MATTER HOW BIG YOU GET, YOU WILL ALWAYS BE MY BABY.

big

Beth Wolfgang

Bordentown, New Jersey

There are always those moments that take you by surprise, when you realize how your baby has grown in leaps and bounds—seemingly overnight! A celebratory yet sentimental design is the perfect way to cherish your child's growth. To create your own design around a single matted black-and-white image, such as the carefree vine shown here, place vellum overtop the layout and draw your design. Then cut out the drawn image, trace it onto cardstock and cut it out. Making your own designs, such as several of the flower shapes shown here, provides the perfect way to use scraps of patterned paper. Hand stitching and puffy fabric paints add dimension and texture.

supplies: Patterned paper (BasicGrey, Imagination Project, KI Memories, SEI); large flower, ghost flowers and letters (Heidi Swapp); buttons, rhinestone brads (SEI); fabric tabs (Scrapworks); flowers (Imagination Project, Queen & Co., SEI); staples; acrylic paint; pigment ink; thread; fabric paint; cardstock

chapter **two**
favorite things

Pacifiers, Play Doh and mismatched mittens, mac 'n cheese and hotdogs have your child's attention. Dinosaurs and dolls, threadbare blankies—these are a few of your toddler's favorite things! Many toddlers find something they like and stick with it, be it a preference in food, color, cartoon or toy, all for the reassurance of comfort and security. Rejoice in your child's blossoming personality as you discover the things that make your child tick. Toddlerhood becomes more and more like Christmas as you enjoy the fun of "unwrapping" the personality behind your little person. Help your child see how unique and wonderfully made he or she is through scrapbook pages that capture these first favorites of your toddler's world.

special juice

Tonia Borrosch

Honeoye Falls, New York

Guilty pleasures now and then make for favorite treats that receive a treasured status in your child's mind, as is evident by Tonia's son savoring every last sip of his "special juice!" Combine an assortment of circular and polka dot patterned papers to achieve an effervescent cheerfulness on your layout, or even circle punch some of the patterns and use the bubbly bursts of color to frame images of your child enjoying his treat.

supplies: Patterned paper, letter stickers, ribbon, rub-ons (Arctic Frog); brads; circle punch; corner rounder; pen; cardstock; Times New Roman font (Microsoft)

gum chewing gurus

Alecia Ackerman Grimm

Atlanta, Georgia

Make your children's favorite pastimes the star of the show on a funky, fabulous creation. Round the edges of your photos for a light-hearted look, while patterned paper frames and cardstock matting need similar curves for double the fun. Handcut arrows in varying sizes can lead from your focal photo into your close-up accent images for a playful approach. Repeat the lines of the arrows by running the cardstock frame off the page for repetition and kinesthetic flow. Alecia alternated rub-on letters and chipboard letters in her title for more viewing pleasure.

supplies: Patterned paper (SEI); chipboard letters (Heidi Swapp, Scenic Route); rub-on letters and numbers (Making Memories); pigment ink; pen; cardstock

color me silly

Rita Shimniok
Cross Plains, Wisconsin

Your child's favorite sweets are even more fun when they can turn their tongue a different color. To play up the theme of a favorite treat, cover chipboard letters in your title with the actual food wrappers and then cover all of the letters with dimensional glaze, as Rita did here with blue raspberry Dum Dum wrappers. Cutting around the outside borders of the patterned papers adds further visual excitement on your page with the negative space created by the design. Machine stitching in a twisting pattern elicits a carefree flow on any layout, while lending texture.

supplies: Patterned paper (BasicGrey, Bo-Bunny); chipboard letters (Heidi Swapp, Making Memories, Pressed Petals); chipboard accents (BasicGrey); rub-ons (Creative Imaginations, EK Success); dimensional glaze; brads; buttons (Junkitz); acrylic paint; ribbon (Michaels); thread; candy wrapper; pen; cardstock

Vicki Boutin
Burlington, Ontario, Canada

What are your toddler's favorite incentives? Be it sticker, trinket or marshmallow treat, a page such as Vicki's is a fun way to document your child's priceless motivations. When creating a layout where the photos are packed with colors, choose softer shades from your images to pull out for the background, and keep your layout from being overwhelmed in distracting colors. Use patterned papers that incorporate the colors from the photos in small doses around the page. Vibrant accents, such as chipboard letters and heart embellishments, give the page a burst of cheer.

supplies: Patterned paper, chipboard letters and shapes (Imagination Project); letter stickers (EK Success); brad (Making Memories); star (unknown); dye ink; sandpaper; pen; cardstock

dipsy

Natalie Bensimhon
Easton, Pennsylvania

Favorite TV show characters also make for favorite naptime companions, as Natalie's dreamy design illustrates. Natalie included her child in the TV character line-up by using cardstock arrows to point to her own little stand-in. Use patterned papers and colors that reflect the elements of your child's favorite show, as Natalie did with the cloud patterned paper and character colors of cardstock. Using a pen to make a unifying pattern throughout the layout is another easy and inexpensive way to create movement and definition.

supplies: Patterned paper (Dream Street); chipboard letters (Pressed Petals); pen; cardstock

got chalk?

Alecia Ackerman Grimm

Atlanta, Georgia

Sometimes a clean slate and piece of chalk are all your toddler needs for hours of entertainment, as Alecia's art-inspired two-page spread attests. Choose a background that mimics the look of your child with his or her favorite medium. Alecia chose distressed, impressionistic papers to coordinate with her child's chalk, and used a white gel pen on black paper to repeat the chalk-on-chalkboard style from her photos. Thematic quotes are a simple yet sentimental way to frame your photos or other page elements. Unify your layouts by creating a mirror-image effect switching the position of the patterned-paper border on each side of the spread.

supplies: Patterned paper (BasicGrey, Die Cuts With A View, Scenic Route); letter stickers (Scenic Route); quote stickers, rub-on letters (KI Memories); dye ink; pen; staples

CELEBRATION

RECORD ANY NOTEWORTHY OCCURENCES--DESCRIBE AT LENGTH

| JAN | FEB | MAR | APR | MAY | JUN |
| JUL | AUG | SEP | OCT | NOV | DEC |

1	17
2	18
3	19
4	20
5	21
6	22
7	23
8	24
9	25
10	26
11	27
12	28
13	29
14	30
15	31
16	*

0 74427 17247 3

joy and delight on Kaiti's birthday

KAITI'S

BEST birthday GIFT

sing

best birthday gift

Kim Kesti
Phoenix, Arizona

Favorite birthday gifts hold a treasured place in your child's memories and should be celebrated on joyful pages. Choose patterned papers and ephemera with words that evoke the emotion of your photos. To keep a girly page from becoming overbearingly pink, add complementary lime green accents and use the negative space of a white background to add its own dynamic. Adding a circle of rhinestones around an acrylic word embellishment is a great way to provide further festivity.

supplies: Patterned paper (A2Z Essentials); scalloped cardstock (Bazzill); journaling tag (7 Gypsies); letter stickers (Doodlebug); round letters (Li'l Davis); flower clip (Creative Imaginations); rhinestone accent (Heidi Swapp); acrylic square accent (KI Memories); cardstock

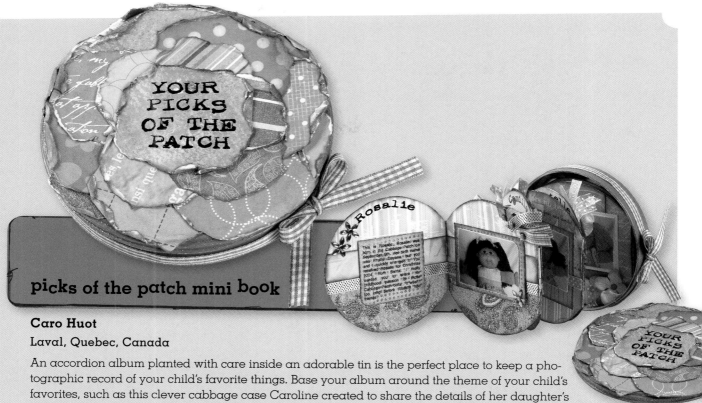

picks of the patch mini book

Caro Huot
Laval, Quebec, Canada

An accordion album planted with care inside an adorable tin is the perfect place to keep a photographic record of your child's favorite things. Base your album around the theme of your child's favorites, such as this clever cabbage case Caroline created to share the details of her daughter's Cabbage Patch Doll collection. A two-page spread is ideal for showcasing images of each item on one page with journaling on the opposing side to share the story behind each special doll. Caroline painted her tin box green for thematic effect, then varnished with glitter glaze for added interest.

supplies: Mini album, metal tin (Autumn Leaves); patterned paper (Adorn It, Anna Griffin, Autumn Leaves, BasicGrey, Chatterbox, Creative Imaginations, DDDesigns 7, Imagination Project, KI Memories, My Mind's Eye, Paper Loft, Prima, Scenic Route, SEI); rub-on letters (Bobarbo); ribbon (American Crafts, May Arts, Offray); flower jewels (unknown); flowers (Prima, Queen & Co.); brads; sequins; rhinestones; acrylic paint; glitter varnish (Delta); chalk; cardstock

cute baseball girl

Sandra Hicks
San Antonio, Texas

Before your junior sports fanatic makes the hall of fame, record the beginnings of his or her sports career-in-the-making on a light-hearted, energetic page. Zig-zag stitching is perfect for mimicking stitched baseball seams, while rickrack reinforces the look. Create a thematic ball for your child's favorite sports pastime by painting chipboard circles to coordinate with your page, and add playful polka-dot accents for repetition. For a feminine touch, a pink background with an assortment of pink painted chipboard letters is sure to be a hit.

supplies: Patterned paper (American Crafts, Making Memories); chipboard letters (Heidi Swapp, Pressed Petals); chipboard words (Heidi Swapp); acrylic paint; chipboard accents (Heidi Swapp, Magistical Memories); brads; paper clip; ribbon (American Crafts); rickrack (Karen Foster); thread; pen; cardstock; Arial Narrow font (Microsoft)

darth tater & spud trooper

Barbara Pfeffer
Omaha, Nebraska

One of the many joys of parenthood—the cool toys you now have an excuse to purchase. Play up the theme of any toy by pulling the colors of the favorite items onto your layout. Barbara chose black and white to enhance the drama between Darth Tater and Spud Trooper. Brown brad accents adhering black and white photo turns add just a hint of warmth to the page and tie the background together with the photos.

supplies: Patterned paper, photo turns (Junkitz); letter stickers (Doodlebug); brads; corner rounder; cardstock; Verdana Ref font (Microsoft)

the drill

Maria Gallardo-Williams
Cary, North Carolina

Sometimes the most surprising items become your child's favorite plaything. Even more surprising can be the ways they discover to use their favorite toys for hours of creative entertainment! Depth, dimension and visual excitement abound on Maria's layout. Brads create a 3-D square and add a hardware effect to play up the theme of the page. Maria formed her title into the illusion of a square, setting an L-shaped arrangement against a square background, allowing your eye to fill in the lines.

supplies: Patterned paper (7 Gypsies); letter stickers (Imagination Project); rub-ons (EK Success); die-cut shapes (Legacy Paper); brads; dye ink; cardstock; Batik Regular font (Internet download)

fun Times in mom's car

BEEP

beep

Marie Cox

Raleigh, North Carolina

Sometimes an image of your toddler in action simply speaks for itself, as is the case with this photo of Marie's son having a ball exploring Mom's car. A stark black background makes a dynamic stage for your photo to shine. A single strip of vibrant patterned paper is layered over several tags and envelopes. Letter stickers and rub-on letters provide the only text on this charismatic page, and add visual excitement to the simple-shape arrangement.

supplies: Patterned paper (Chatterbox); letter stickers, rub-ons (Making Memories); envelope (Bazzill); tags (unknown); stitches (Li'l Davis); cardstock

July 2006

HER FAVORITES

discover (di-skuv-er) v. To notice or learn so... or effort

MYGIRL

AMERICAN DRAGON
bread-n-butter
flip flops   pink popsicles   nightgowns
Lilo and Stitch   BARBIES
Maddie bike
OLD NAVY   Faith Hill
Stouffers Mac-n-Cheese

her favorites

Valerie Fowler

Monroe, Michigan

Peanut butter and jelly, macaroni necklaces made from string—these just may be a few of your child's favorite things! Document your child's personal Top Ten, listing favorite treats, videos and play things. This digital layout creates depth by giving the illusion of patterned-paper layers behind a large adorable photo. Use a variety of fonts and type sizes to give added energy to random favorites arranged playfully at the bottom of the page.

supplies: Digital patterned paper, layered paper, "my girl" tab (Jen Wilson); definition strip, twill tape (Digi Chick); Bookman Old Style, Century Gothic fonts (Microsoft); CheltPress Trial, Jailbird Jenna, Punch Label fonts (Internet download)

baby doll

Vicki Boutin
Burlington, Ontario, Canada

A child's character develops through play, as Vicki illustrates here on this adoring look at a three-year-old's nurturing instincts beginning to bloom. To achieve a similar look of gentle strength on your own pages, combine the bold intensity of patterned papers with stamps in a complementary theme. Use colored pencils to enliven the stamped images, as Vicki did with her build-your-own flower stamps set to the right of the image. A scalloped edge along patterned paper is a simple way to lend feminine flair to any layout.

supplies: Patterned paper (Heidi Grace); stamps (Gel-a-tins); dye ink; brads (Queen & Co.); colored pencils; pen; cardstock

dr. stella

Alecia Ackerman Grimm
Atlanta, Georgia

Dramatic play not only helps your child better understand his or her world, but it's also the perfect window for parents to get in on the fun. A thematic page dedicated to your toddler's favorite dress-up dramas can easily be established through one playful photo of your child in costume. Alecia matted her photo onto cardstock and then rematted it onto themed patterned paper. Smudged edges around the image give a contrasting playful glimpse into an imaginary world, while notebook paper journaling strips further the childhood charm.

supplies: Patterned paper, brads, stickers (Around the Block); chipboard letters (Heidi Swapp); notebook paper; pen; cardstock

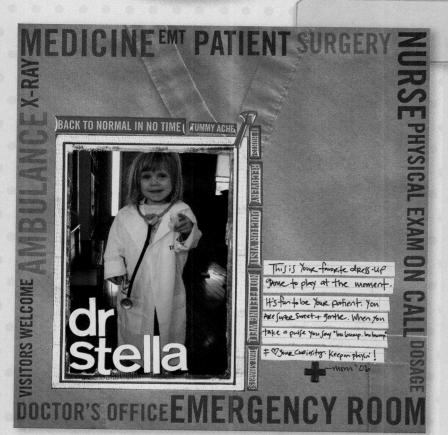

43

incognito

Tonia Borrosch
Honeoye Falls, New York

Your child's favorite silly sessions need a page of their own. Use an assortment of patterned chipboard letters to lend a whimsical finesse to your page design, and accentuate the letters with ribbons and spiral clips for extra fun. An enlarged photo of your child at his silliest packs a powerful punch on any page, and calls for very little embellishment. Tonia created her own thematic embellishment by making a letter "Q" with her circle cutter and adding an epoxy arrow accent to emphasize the question mark in the center.

supplies: Patterned paper, chipboard letters, epoxy accents (KI Memories); brads, velvet stickers (Making Memories); ribbon (Offray); photo turns, spiral clip (Making Memories); circle cutter; notebook paper; pen; cardstock; Times New Roman font (Microsoft)

mountain

Maria Gallardo-Williams
Cary, North Carolina

Whether your child's favorite sneaky thing to do is getting into the cat food, picking plants from your flowerbed, or hauling woodchips in a dumptruck, as Maria's son enjoys, create a dynamic layout to laugh at together with your child in the years to come. A multitude of colorful circles set against solid, dark blocks along the top and bottom of a page make for a powerful contrast and a look of strength. Maria chose letter stamps with a a strong font and used paint to stamp the title. A metal-rimmed tag and a trio of brads repeat the look of the patterned paper background.

supplies: Patterned paper (SEI); brads, letter stamps, spiral clip, tag (Making Memories); circle sticker (Club Scrap); acrylic paint; mesh (Magic Mesh); transparency; cardstock

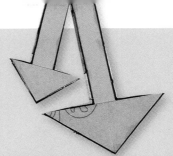

For the Love of

TRAINS

PLAY

FUN

ENJOY

This was the best gift we ever bought for Ethan. His train set might be scattered all over the house, but he plays with it more than anything else. I love to hear the stories he comes up with, bringing these little train characters to life, exercising that big imagination. In our house, we've got a whole lot of love for these trains.

for the love of trains

Courtney Walsh
Winnebago, Illinois

No album of your child's would be complete without a tribute to his or her most prized possession, as Courtney created on this digital salute to her son's trains. The illusion of a smudged ink frame is an easy way to give any page a masculine feel while adding a rough-and-tumble finesse. The look transfers easily to traditional paper layouts by simply inking your boundaries. Shadows beneath accent images lend depth to the layout, accomplishing the same effect as foam adhesive spacers would to paper projects. Chunky fonts are a great way to repeat the look of your toddler's chubby hands.

supplies: Digital paper, frame (Two Peas in a Bucket); Goudy Old Style, Times New Roman fonts (Microsoft)

superhero obsession

Greta Hammond

Goshen, Indiana

Whether your child's alter ego is a superhero, a superstar, or perhaps a dog or cat, children sometimes love to pretend to be someone or something else, and costumes only enhance the fun. To incorporate several dynamic photos of your child at play into a single layout, a two-page spread provides the perfect solution, allowing each image to have room to stand on its own. A thematic emblem, such as Greta's cut patterned paper stars, unifies the two pages and divides the journaling into two balanced sections for symmetry.

supplies: Patterned paper (Scenic Route); chipboard letters, brads (Making Memories); rub-on letters (Imagination Project); pen; cardstock; Times New Roman font (Microsoft)

everyday superhero

Maria Gallardo-Williams

Cary, North Carolina

Uncommon commitment to a favorite outfit, be it a princess dress, dance recital costume, or a super-hero costume deserves to be remembered on a special layout. An enlarged photo of your child performing everyday activities in his or her daily costume of choice makes for a hilarious memory on your layout, while a close-up accent photo furthers the fun. Large, comic-style, chubby letter stickers play up the hilarity on your page, especially when arranged off-kilter.

supplies: Patterned paper, letter stickers, accent stickers (Sonburn); cardstock; Century Gothic font (Microsoft)

Kelly Goree
Shelbyville, Kentucky

Your child's love affair with literature is a bond you'll nurture in him or her always. Be sure to document this special relationship from the beginning, as Kelly demonstrates with her son's first solo attempt at reading. A color-blocked layout coordinates well with the simplicity of primary colors on the design. Negative space between the blocks of vibrant cardstock and unobtrusive patterned paper create dynamic lines of definition throughout the page, while providing a stark white frame for a row of photos set together. A combination of lowercase and capital white letter stickers emphasize the look of child's play.

supplies: Patterned paper (Daisy D's); letter stickers (Chatterbox); dye ink; corner rounder; cardstock

---

creativity

Amanda Williams
Tucson, Arizona

Less is often more when capturing the beauty of childhood in its purest form. Amanda let a row of simple-shaped, die-cut flowers pose as the main embellishment on this free-spirited design celebrating her child's favorite artistic toy. A few basic strips of cardstock along the borders and a single patterned-paper band to separate photos are all that is needed to create a colorful and carefree layout. A rainbow-colored ribbon adds texture and ties the design together.

supplies: Patterned paper (Chatterbox); letter stickers (Me & My Big Ideas); die-cut flowers (Urban Lily); ribbon (Wal-Mart); dye ink (Stampin' Up); cardstock

On the layout: *June 2006* · *DANCE* · *cute, darling, my sweet little girl. Lovable, fun, always making everyone laugh. Full of smiles and so happy, most of the time. Affectionate, talkative and outgoing. A living doll who I adore and love.* · *Chloe loves dancing in her cute ballet outfit she got for Halloween!*

dance

Suzy Plantamura

Laguna Niguel, California

photo by Tara Whitney Photography, Mission Vejo, California

Having a child helps parents remember to find time for the simple joys of life. On this page, Suzy's daughter enjoys dancing in her room while wearing her favorite tutu. By enlarging a favorite image of your child in her element, a layout instantly focuses on the photo. However, in this photo Suzy's daughter was set off to the far left of the image. A circle cut from patterned paper formed a perfect frame around her child, keeping her the center of attention. Circle stickers embellished with rhinestones dance with delicate flowers around the zoom-lens frame for a page filled with frills and femininity. A semi-circle cut from coordinating patterned paper provides dramatic effect and bold repetition of shape in the background.

supplies: Patterned paper, chipboard letters, round stickers (Creative Imaginations); ribbon (Making Memories); flowers (Prima); brads (Queen & Co.); rhinestones (Heidi Swapp, Making Memories); circle cutter; dye ink; marker

pillow

Nic Howard
Pukekohe, New Zealand

Capture the items that bring great comfort to your little one on soft and snuggly scrapbook pages. Nic's quiet flow of die-cut flowers cascades down the page to frame a gentle black-and-white image in playful beauty. Stamped floral images provide a contrasting aesthetic to the paper flower arrangement and add to the carefree movement. Nic used glitter paint to add a dreamy dazzle to her die-cut flowers.

supplies: Patterned paper, punch out flowers (Sassafras Lass); chipboard letters (Heidi Swapp); ribbon (Heidi Grace); stamps (Autumn Leaves); dye ink; glitter paint; thread; pen; cardstock

49

Marie Cox
Raleigh, North Carolina

A babe and his paci create an unexplainable bond. Marie captures the joy on her son's face with his favorite security item, and expresses the dilemma parents face at the thought of taking away such a treasured item. For a bold, blocked look on your own pages, arrange all page elements into the shape of a square and set it against a powerful color of cardstock for the background. Pick a background color that is less intense than the photo to ensure the photo maintains the focus of the page. A simple sticker accent at the base of the arrangement balances out the photo.

supplies: Patterned paper (American Crafts); chipboard heart (Heidi Swapp); chipboard letters (Creative Imaginations); sticker accent (7 Gypsies); cardstock

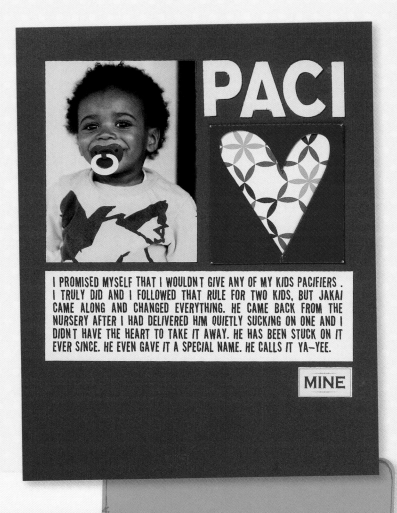

PACI

I PROMISED MYSELF THAT I WOULDN'T GIVE ANY OF MY KIDS PACIFIERS. I TRULY DID AND I FOLLOWED THAT RULE FOR TWO KIDS, BUT JAKAI CAME ALONG AND CHANGED EVERYTHING. HE CAME BACK FROM THE NURSERY AFTER I HAD DELIVERED HIM QUIETLY SUCKING ON ONE AND I DIDN'T HAVE THE HEART TO TAKE IT AWAY. HE HAS BEEN STUCK ON IT EVER SINCE. HE EVEN GAVE IT A SPECIAL NAME. HE CALLS IT YA-YEE.

MINE

button

Sheila Doherty
Coeur d'Alene, Idaho

Draw attention to the details of your toddler's favorite quirks by creating a swirl of cut papers, as Sheila employed here to denote her son's adorable obsession of sticking his finger in his belly button while sucking his thumb. Overlap the beginning and end points of the swirl overtop the photo to guide the eye to the little nuances that may otherwise become overlooked. A playful way to lend nostalgic cuteness is to incorporate thematic embellishments into your title, as Sheila demonstrates here with an actual button tied into her title of the same name.

supplies: Patterned paper (SEI); letter rub-ons (Scrapworks); rub-on accents (Doodlebug); ribbon (American Crafts); paper floss (Karen Foster); corner rounder; cardstock; CK Brownie font (Creating Keepsakes)

button

01.03.06

snuggle

Vicki Boutin

Burlington, Ontario, Canada

For a quick and inexpensive layout packed full of sentiment and softness, invent your own patterned paper by hand-drawing an overall background design and title with pen, and then using colored pencils in shades from your photographs. A patterned paper frame was the only extra Vicki added to this endearing, childhood celebration of a boy and his favorite bear.

supplies: Patterned paper (Scenic Route); pen; colored pencils; cardstock

51

thumbsucker

Dana Swords
Doswell, Virginia

Whether your child is addicted to the pacifier, a favorite blankie, or even her thumb, toddlerhood habits are definitely hard to break, but easy to commemorate on lighthearted layouts. Combine a couple images of your child in action with a favorite habit, then maintain the focus on the photos by employing only two patterned papers in overlapped blocks about the page. Dana tied her photos together by aligning the background railing in her photos to pull the eye along. A striped pattern paper used in the background is balanced by free-flowing flowers for contrast.

supplies: Patterned paper (Chatterbox); letter stickers (SEI); foam stamps (Making Memories); acrylic paint; concho; fabric (unknown); dye ink; cardstock

wooby

Becky Heisler
Waupaca, Wisconsin

Record the story behind your child's favorite security item on a soft, sentimental layout. Becky documented the tale behind her son's "security doily,"—a.k.a., Wooby. A black-and-white photograph lends a classic, timeless quality to a page composed of quiet, distressed patterned papers. A cut patterned-paper circle zooms in on the subject and provides cohesiveness with the rest of the layout. Handwritten journaling enhances the sentimental value.

supplies: Patterned paper (BasicGrey); letter stickers (American Crafts); shell accents (unknown); inscription pen; dye ink; pens; cardstock

Joshua's best blanket

It's a good thing you can't read yet Joshua, because it pains me to write this. This is a photo of you and "Best" - your 'best blanket'. Best was your companion in all you did. Slept with you, snuggled with you, watched t.v., made tents, was your super hero cape many a time. "He" even went to preschool with you. You were buddies! And then we moved. And somehow Best got left behind. I know he was at the house when the movers were there - you left him on the floor. My guess is that the cleaners got him mixed up in their towels and by the time we realized it, it was too late. Night after night in the new house you asked me to unpack more boxes to look for Best and my heart broke because I knew he wasn't there. I had dreams about finding that blanket for you! I searched the internet and Tommy Hilfiger Outlet shops across America with no luck. We have since found a similar blanket that you have aptly named "Cousin Best", but it's just not the same. Six months later you still ask where Best is and my heart still breaks when you do.

'best' friends

best blanket

Stacy McFadden
Park Orchards, Victoria, Australia

A boy and his blanket are a bond no one can sever...even long after blankie is lost, packed away, or has become a single thread from overuse. Create cuddly keepsakes of your little one and his favorite fabric wrapped up on a page of their own. Stacy used a frayed edge denim background on this computer-generated creation, and then "cut" her title letters from the background for a cohesive, all-boy look. Hand-drawn elements on an electronic tablet, such as the tags, metal label holder, photo turns and flowers on Stacy's design, can all be saved as brushes to be easily "stamped" onto future layouts.

supplies: Digital background (Digital Design Essentials); denim and stitching (Scrapbook Graphics); bookplate, photo turns, tags (artist's own design); American Typewriter, Penstyle fonts (Internet download); Impact font (Microsoft)

chapter **three**
family & friends

How rich is the child's life filled with family and friends to love and to be loved by! Whether it's fishing trips with Grandpa or just making a mess with a first favorite friend, life's events are always more fun when they can be shared with someone special. Help your child remember the many faces familiar to their childhood through timeless page creations that pay tribute to your toddler's sense of community. Relationships with grandparents, playmates, care providers and siblings all play important roles in your child's social and emotional development and build treasured spots in their heart from the very beginning. Scrapbook your toddler's world of friends and family members on pages that will keep these relationships fondly remembered and always alive in spirit.

daddy and you

Vicki Boutin
Burlington, Ontario, Canada

How precious the love between father and son, as Vicki shows here on this fun-packed design. A loving image of your child with his dad deserves a dynamic placement on your layout. Vicki matted her focal-photo with a masculine yet whimsical patterned paper. A longer piece of patterned paper, like the paper on the right, is a great space for including numerous accent photos to showcase your child's special relationship with Dad.

supplies: Patterned paper, chipboard letters (Scenic Route); chipboard shapes (Making Memories); brads; pigment ink; pen; cardstock

unconditional

Tonia Borrosch
Honeoye Falls, New York

The way a child clings to a parent for security fills a parent's heart with unconditional love. Tonia's simplistic yet sentimental page tugs at the heartstrings, as she allows a powerful image of her son with his daddy to speak for itself. Definition rub-ons are a simple way to place text on your design, with buttons layered on top for texture and color. Try embellishing a ready-made thematic die-cut with a gem and rub-ons, or photo corners and photo turns.

supplies: Patterned paper (Provo Craft); gem accent (Darice); photo turn (Autumn Leaves); buttons (unknown); square with heart accent (My Mind's Eye); photo corner; narrative rub-ons (Karen Russell); pen; cardstock

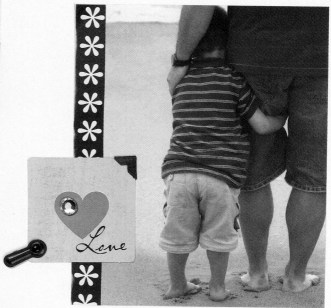

giggle (gig'-el) 1. a giddy laughter 2. laughter in a silly or nervous manner 3. often accompanying secrets among young girls

being together

This picture makes me smile! Daddy was trying to get a headshot of me, but you kept walking into the picture! After moving you several times, I finally pulled you close and gave you a snuggle! That's all you wanted... 30 seconds of my time. And daddy was good enough to capture it!

July 15, 2006

XOXOXOX

LOVE

this girl

Amy Farnsworth

Brighton, Colorado

Words that can adequately describe the bond between mother and child are hard to find. But playful patterns, sassy fun colors and whimsical embellishments are great tools of communication on a mother/daughter tribute. Flowers accentuated with buttons lend simplistic delight and freewheeling fun, while glitter-enhanced chipboard words and love-themed rub-ons express the exhilaration and joy in this most special bond. A black-and-white image stands out against the layout's bold colors, yet pulls together nicely with metal frames painted for emphasis and embellished with metallic rub-ons.

supplies: Patterned paper, letter stickers, die-cut flowers (Urban Lily); acrylic letters (KI Memories); metal accents (In a Blink of an Eye); chipboard word (Pressed Petals); oversized button (Bazzill); buttons (Autumn Leaves); rub-ons (Autumn Leaves, Craf-T, Creative Imaginations, Scenic Route); silk flower (Doodlebug); definition sticker (Making Memories); decorative scissors; ribbon (May Arts); jewel accents (Heidi Swapp); acrylic paint; cardstock; Century Gothic font (Microsoft)

mom, he's bothering me

Barbara Pfeffer

Omaha, Nebraska

To older siblings everywhere, little brothers seem to have a gift for transforming from treasured friend to pesky annoyance. Barbara designed this layout to pay tribute to the close relationship shared between this brother and sis, despite the typical episodes involving the brother-as-pest. To capture the same lighthearted look at love on your own pages, follow Barbara's example, employing patterned papers that embrace the snips-and-snails attitude of your own little boy, and setting several of your title letters off-kilter to play-up the mischievous theme.

supplies: Patterned paper, letter stickers (BasicGrey); chipboard letters (Li'l Davis); corner punch; thread; AL Worm Machine font (Autumn Leaves)

From the moment I found out I was carrying a boy, I knew the day would come, the day when your sweet baby brother turned into a pesky little brother. Well sweetie, that day is now. Even though you are almost 4 years apart in age, you and Nick have always had a close relationship, probably because you were both home together while Toria was at school all day. But despite your closeness, or maybe because of it, you seem to be bearing the brunt of Nick's peskiness. He is constantly trying to wrestle you, or hit you, or jump on you while you're watching TV. But honey, try to remember that all that bothering is just his way of trying to get your attention. Now that you are in school all day, he misses his "Wessy". Many days he watches for the bus to bring you home. He loves you so much. And I know that you love him too, even though he bothers you sometimes!

10.08.05

playtime with daddy

Stacy McFadden

Park Orchards, Victoria, Australia

Digital designs deliver timeless sentiment in traditional style, as Stacy shows on this computer-generated creation celebrating the time her son was blessed to spend with his daddy, now passed away. Special pages to help your child remember treasured times with loved ones are so important. A Wacom pen tablet is a simple electronic tool for drawing your own title letters directly onto a layout. Then color in each inside section with the wand tool. Use the pen tool to add your own playful borders, or other special features like the curved text Stacy added to the bottom of her page.

supplies: Digital background paper, black ribbon, felt trim, folio tab, star (Digital Design Essentials); rickrack, stitched circle (Shabby Princess); blue and red stitching (Scrapbook Graphics); string tabs (Designer Digitals); doodled stars, index tab, title lettering (artist's own design); image editing software (Adobe); Dymo, Jayne Print fonts (Internet download)

BOYS

WILL BE BOYS!
I knew from day one that you would be
Daddy's boy. I never had a chance.
Your Daddy couldn't wait to come
home from work and play with his new
buddy. Even to this day I am a
temporary playmate until Daddy
comes home. That's okay. I know you
are loved. More than you'll ever know.

HAVE FUN   PLAY HARD   HAVE FUN   PLAY HARD   HA

EVERYDAY ADVENTURES
EVERYDAY LIFE
remember

PLAY HARD

boys will be boys

Cindy Smith
Knoxville, Maryland

There's just something about the father/son bond that makes a mother's heart melt and a child's ambition grow. Create an all-star tribute to your special boys as a celebration of the role a daddy plays in his son's life. Cindy chose a rough-and-tumble design using distressed cardstock and grunge-effect patterned papers to emphasize the boyish charm. Inked and smudged edges around elements complete the boyishly masculine look. The illusion of stitching around the title letters mimics the look of the team monogram hats, while a metal star accent repeats the shape in the journaling background.

supplies: Patterned paper, die-cut accents, stickers (Sweetwater); twill (Maya Road); ribbon (Offray); star clip (Hillcreek); chalk ink; adhesive foam; cardstock

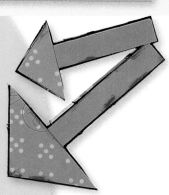

Memories of childhood
may someday fade,

but never the special
games we played.

Though our tea party days
will come to an end,

you're always my sister,
always my friend.

Unknown

My Sweethearts, February 2006

APRIL

Thank you God for little sisters
They keep us on our toes
They plan with us and laugh with us
And mess up our Legos

God gave me a sister
To teach me about life
She loves and aggravates me
And gives me strength and strife

Thank you God for little sisters
They are special as can be
Don't mess with my little sister
Or you'll have to mess with me

Unknown

sisterhood 2005 mini album

Amanda Williams

Tucson, Arizona

On days when young siblings are feeling blue, a sweet and sentimental celebration of family is a handy investment to have around. Having two daughters only 18 months apart, Amanda designed this through-the-year mini album to pay tribute to the special friendship shared between sisters. Create your own book of happy times spent with good friends or family utilizing month stickers to lend a calendar effect. Simple heart and circle punches create adorable accents in a plethora of patterns and prints.

supplies: Spiral album (7 Gypsies); patterned paper, coasters, month tabs (Imagination Project); letter stickers (SEI); brads; decorative punches (EK Success); dye ink; ribbons (Doodlebug, May Arts, Wal-Mart); circle punch; pen; cardstock

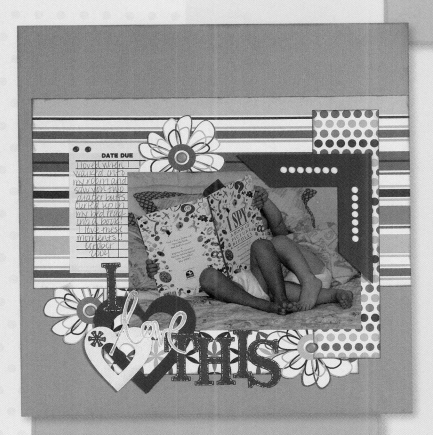

i love this

Kim Moreno
Tucson, Arizona

Twins take sibling closeness to a whole new level, as Kim illustrates here on this bright and bold page. To emphasize family closeness on your own page creations, follow Kim's example by overlapping title words and elements for a look that melds many pieces into one cohesive whole. For dramatic impact on otherwise average letter stickers, add the effect of stitches or other designs around the inside edges with a white pen. This also helps the letters stand out from a busy background. Stamp a word in a flowing font onto white cardstock, cut out the stamped word and overlap it with the other title words and accents.

supplies: Patterned paper, letter stickers (American Crafts); chipboard accents (Magistical Memories); "love" stamp (Heidi Swapp); pigment ink; brads; journaling card (local library); pen; cardstock

brotherly love

Kelly Goree
Shelbyville, Kentucky

Boys tend to have a special amount of energy and wild will that oftentimes calls for extreme measures if you wish to capture a photo of them together. Kelly created this humorous design to laugh at the formality of staging these photos for her layout—the only way to hold the three brothers still at the same time. A large hand-cut heart is a charming yet bold background element to help images pop off the page, while hand stitching in several colors lends texture and childhood sentiment. To repeat the look with masculine edge, use wire accents. Kelly strung the covered chipboard hearts together with wire and curled the ends to add a bit of whimsy.

supplies: Patterned paper, chipboard shapes (BasicGrey); letter stickers (BasicGrey, Chatterbox); wire; embroidery floss; dye ink; cardstock

Since Jakai was born you two have been inseparable. You are so patient with him and love to mother him. You play with him when he's bored and always make sure he is included in things we do. I hope that you always stay this close with each other.

Marie Cox
Raleigh, North Carolina

Celebrate the unbreakable bond between siblings on a simple design like Marie's, which communicates the love found in family friendships with minimal décor. Kraft paper background creates a raw, earthy feel, for a look that touches on the pure essence of love shared between siblings. Rub-on accents lend a colorful edge yet allow photos to stand out. Balance the look of smaller images with a pronounced title, as Marie demonstrates here with an oversized stamp.

supplies: Patterned paper (Autumn Leaves); rub-ons (Chatterbox); photo corners (Heidi Swapp); digital brush (Two Peas in a Bucket); Kraft cardstock

push

Jennifer Gallacher
American Fork, Utah

Want to highlight one sibling in particular while celebrating a special sibling relationship? Follow Jennifer's lead, as she features her youngest son on this strong composition of wisdom and whimsy. Using the portrait mode on her camera, Jennifer was able to keep the youngest son in focus in her photo, while still capturing the essence of her oldest son in the background. To achieve the same solid look at the bottom of your own designs, use a square punch on your journaling and photos and arrange the blocks into a grid. By alternating photos with journaling squares, visual excitement abounds on the page and keeps the eye moving.

supplies: Patterned paper (Chatterbox); brads, letter stamps, stamping ink (Karen Foster); chipboard letters, clear stars (Heidi Swapp); chipboard accent (Li'l Davis); snaps (Making Memories); staples; cardstock; Century Gothic font (Microsoft)

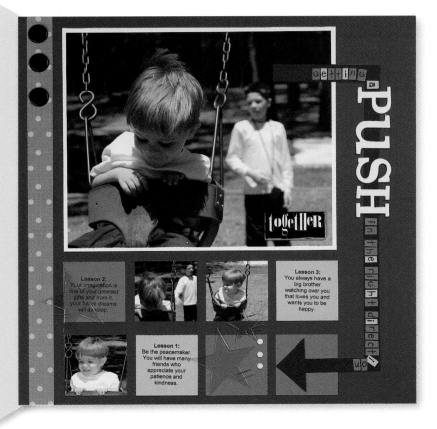

getting

PUSH
in the right direction

together

Lesson 2: Your imagination is one of your greatest gifts and from it, your future dreams will develop.

Lesson 3: You always have a big brother watching over you that loves you and wants you to be happy.

Lesson 1: Be the peacemaker. You will have many friends who appreciate your patience and kindness.

The love you two share never ceases to amaze me! When Brinley was born I expected Drew to act out in anger, but he didn't. He took to his little sister immediately and still continues to help and protect her any chance he gets – well, almost!

June 2006

you're what *dreams* are made of...

Cherish

Amy Farnsworth

Brighton, Colorado

Loving moments exchanged between siblings warm a mother's heart and inspires her to create, much like Amy did here on this sweet and sentimental page of sibling love. For images where two heads come together in a tender kiss or embrace, use the point of contact to launch the shape of a heart in your background. Amy simply cut this large heart accent from a rich crimson patterned paper to emphasize the depth of love. Ready-made journaling blocks, requiring little embellishment, fill in the lower portion of the heart outline with strips of printed journaling. Repeat the shape with clear acrylic hearts overlapping on a chipboard label.

supplies: Patterned paper (BasicGrey, Chatterbox); chipboard letters (Provo Craft); chipboard accents (BasicGrey, Maya Road); rub-on (Autumn Leaves); flower (Bazzill); ribbon (Making Memories, May Arts); clear hearts, decorative tape (Heidi Swapp); pin, quote sticker (Making Memories); brads; embroidery floss; Century Gothic font (Microsoft)

fishing with papa

Cindy Smith

Knoxville, Maryland

The joy a grandchild receives in learning a passion shared by a grandparent deserves a special layout. This two-page design commemorates the passing of the torch, or in Cindy's son's case, the fish. For a dynamic effect, print your journaling and leave spaces for colorful word stickers you can incorporate into the block. Use coordinating word stickers to establish a border around free-flowing background shapes used for color and visual interest. A large focal-point photo of your child showing pride in a newly learned skill is a great way to balance out photos of the art of learning the activity from a beloved grandparent.

supplies: Patterned paper, brad bars, fishing stickers (Karen Foster); letter stickers (American Crafts, Destination Scrapbook); word stickers (Destination Stickers); wooden letters (Westrim); pigment ink; adhesive foam; corner rounder; cardstock

The journaling block reads:

...between siblings is so special. Breanna and Josiah bonded shortly after he was born. He looks up to her as his big sis. I know that Breanna can get a tad bit frustrated with him, but deep down there is an abundance of LOVE!

10-05

love

Sharon Laakkonen

Superior, Wisconsin

Treasure the tender moments and the special bond between siblings. On this cool and calm page of affection, hand-cut hearts add a sentimental border. Stitch two lines weaving in and out throughout your layout to connect the heart border and illustrate how these two siblings' hearts have intertwined. Tie an otherwise basic journaling block into the design by handwriting emphasized words on coordinating scraps of patterned paper spaces. A stitched row of hearts reinforces the message of love.

supplies: Patterned paper, letter stickers (Imagination Project); thread; pen; cardstock

celebrate life

Leana Lucas
Marlboro, Massachusetts

The little daily life experiences that we share with our loved ones add up to big memories, as is evident on Leana's collage layout, featuring everyday moments of her children celebrating life. Chipboard arrows make for pronounced boundaries on this photo-packed page. By journaling around the outside edges of the photos, you can incorporate heartfelt emotion with minimal space while adding decorative flair. A glitter pen is all that's needed to accentuate chipboard arrows for a hint of sparkle, complementing the zest of life in your photos.

supplies: Cardstock; chipboard arrows (Deluxe Designs); letter stickers (Doodlebug); glitter pen (Sakura); stamping ink (Stampin' Up); pen

grandma brag book mini album

Amanda Williams
Tucson, Arizona

Is there a grandma around who doesn't like to brag about her grandchildren? Help your adoring relative showcase her pride in a tiny 2" x 2" brag book. The album's petite size tucks neatly into a purse, or even pocket, allowing for 24/7 accessibility to the apples of any grandparent's eye. Design your own mini mobile gallery using a teeny cardstock album as your starting point. Paper flowers, stickers, ribbons and colorful buttons provide endless possibilities to the playful décor you can add to augment your photos. Miniscule size—mighty fun!

supplies: Patterned paper (KI Memories, Me & My Big Ideas, My Mind's Eye, Three Bugs in a Rug); pink letter stickers (Scrapworks); buttons, round letter stickers (unknown); flowers (Prima); word accents (7 Gypsies, Scrapworks); ribbon (May Arts); heart punch; dye ink; staples; cardstock

can i take your order?

Kim Moreno
Tucson, Arizona

Games never seem to grow old when a beloved grandpa is involved! Capture special memories of your toddler at play with Grandpa, like Kim features on this thematic page showcasing her daughter's favorite game of "waitress." To make your own diner-like look on a layout, create a large curved arrow and cover with rhinestone brads for the illusion of lights. White pen doodles set around the arrow against a black backdrop further illuminate the look. Embellish a photo corner or other page element with rhinestones for a unified effect of delight throughout the page.

supplies: Patterned paper (Autumn Leaves); chipboard letters and accents (Magistical Memories); rhinestone brads (Making Memories); stamps (Fontwerks, PSX); dye ink; ribbon (Michaels); paperclips; acrylic paint; pen; cardstock

awesome aunt kristy

Amy Farnsworth
Brighton, Colorado

Special aunts deserve a tribute page as touching and tender as the one Amy designed for her children's treasured auntie. Vintage looking papers lend a timeless sentiment to a layout with feminine finesse enhanced by the look of large silk flowers and swirling plumes printed on a transparency. Soft velvety letter stickers give quiet texture to any design, while rhinestone accents add just a hint of sparkle and glam.

supplies: Patterned paper, letter stickers, ribbon, metal accents (Making Memories); silk flowers, rhinestones (Prima); transparency (K&Co.); canvas reinforcers (7 Gypsies); chipboard shapes (Li'l Davis); Century Gothic font (Microsoft); Miss Priss font (Two Peas in a Bucket)

mamaw love

Kim Moreno
Tucson, Arizona

When relatives live far away, pages like the one Kim created to show the bond between her daughter and MaMaw are important treasures that keep the love of family relationships growing across the miles. A black-and-white photo creates a timeless look of love on any page, which contrasts nicely with the joyful colors Kim chose for feminine flair. Cut around the edges of the patterned paper designs to create an eye-catching border, or create your own with a white pen, much like the framed effect Kim added with a dotted design. A simple brad added to the center of colorful photo turns create unique flower embellishments.

supplies: Patterned paper, tags (Three Bugs in a Rug); letter stickers (Doodlebug); clear flowers, photo turns (Magic Scraps); large eyelet (We R Memory Keepers); brads; pen; cardstock

Text within the layout image:

> Who could ask for a better Uncle?
> David has boundless energy for you both,
> is crazy and fun loving. He loves
> spending time with you and is always
> encouraging you to be mischievous. That
> is why he is one of your favourite people!

DAVID

crazy uncle david

Phillipa Campbell

Jerrabomberra, Australia

Life is more fun with a crazy uncle around, as Phillipa's children can attest on this clever combination of childhood play and masculine mayhem. Greens, blues and browns provide a superb color scheme for the layout. A military green background of patterned paper poses a serious weight to a page, which grounds the eye and meshes well with black-and-white photos. Overlay a background of formal flair with stitched blocks of fun and add your own carefree embellishments, much like these matted, patterned paper stars, which Phillipa enhanced with chipboard circle frames for depth and visual contrast.

supplies: Patterned paper (Chatterbox, Daisy D's, SEI); buttons (Chatterbox); star punch (Carl); circle frames (Maya Road); wooden letter (Li'l Davis); thread; tag; ribbon; pen; cardstock

faces of family

Kathy Fesmire
Athens, Tennessee

When your child's loved ones live far away, create connections through this dual-purpose mini album. Serving as both a special home for all your long-distance relatives and a learning tool for your toddler, a CD tin is the perfect size for your child to interact with photos of family members while keeping them close to heart and mind. A pre-made accordion album fits snuggly inside the embellished tin, which you can accentuate with either a female or male flair. Chipboard letters will lend a dimensional edge, while ribbons and buttons add an assortment of textures to appeal to both little eyes and hands.

supplies: Patterned paper, rub-on letters (Paper Studio); circle punch, decorative cutter, flower punch, round tin (EK Success); chipboard letters (Li'l Davis); letter stickers (Doodlebug, EK Success); ribbons (American Crafts); acrylic paint; decoupage medium; buttons (unknown); dye ink; cardstock

e & z

Becky Heisler
Waupaca, Wisconsin

Sometimes friends and family are interchangeable, as is the case with Becky's son and her nephew. Create your own special page designs to showcase your child's extraordinary friendships within your own family. To make your own patterned paper that's sure to complement any scroll or flourish rub-on accent, trace around a chipboard swirl with a variety of colorful pens. Overlap the designs for a free-flowing effect, as Becky demonstrates here. A color photo for her focal-point image shows the warmth between these two cousins, while a strip of black and white photos alongside her journaling illustrates the details of the boys' first sleepover.

supplies: Patterned paper, rub-ons (Adorn It); die-cut letters, punctuation marks (American Crafts); letter stickers (SEI); pen; swirls (traced from Fancy Pants chipboard shape); cardstock

cousins and friends

Courtney Walsh
Winnebago, Illinois

Kissin' cousins couldn't be closer than these sweet family friends Courtney embraces on this page about a close-knit relationship. To use up loads of photos in a single layout, follow Courtney's example in a photo-collage set inside a large cut circle. A larger image incorporated into the design flips up revealing hidden journaling beneath. Bold letter stickers can be used to spell out your subjects' names on opposing sides of the page. Handwrite personality traits for each name, journaling around the circle.

supplies: Patterned paper, letter stickers (Chatterbox); dye ink; Velcro; corner rounder; pen; cardstock

miss carrie

Greta Hammond
Goshen, Indiana

Loving relationships between your child and other caring, non-parental adults lead to forever friendships that will always be part of your child's life. Greta created this tribute to her daughter's beloved childcare provider who is also a treasured friend. Create special pages for the special people in your own child's life, showcasing images of your child with these extended "family" members. Two strips of patterned paper were all that were used on this charming creation, with a single strip of large rickrack embellished with buttons and a chipboard flourish added for texture.

supplies: Patterned paper (American Crafts); chipboard letters (Heidi Swapp); die-cut letters (Provo Craft); chipboard accent (Fancy Pants); buttons (Autumn Leaves); rickrack (May Arts); rub-ons (Chatterbox, K&Co.); flower, sticker (Chatterbox); date stamp (Making Memories); corner rounder; cardstock

m & d

Vicki Boutin
Burlington, Ontario, Canada

Friendships know no age limit, as Vicki's playfully sweet and totally girl layout attests, illustrating the sisterly love between these young playmates. To create your own unique flower embellishments, cut chipboard photo corners to form petals, and set them in place over patterned paper circles. Adorn the centers with a cheerful button and then simply add stems below. For dimensional fun, Vicki wrapped a strip of brown cardstock around a pen, making the spiral body for the clever butterfly embellishment. Use a pen to create the antennae and to add dots of motion along the bottom.

supplies: Patterned paper, chipboard accents (Imagination Project); rub-ons (Scrapworks); buttons (unknown); pen; cardstock

friends

Greta Hammond
Goshen, Indiana

Girlfriends play an important role in the lives of females. Rejoice in your child's first friendship through a lovely and lively layout, like the one Greta designed around her daughter's little friend. Use a black-and-white photo for your focal-point image, contrasting it against full color accent photos. Rub-on floral accents with the look of handstitching will give your page a nostalgic comfort.

supplies: Patterned paper (BasicGrey); chipboard letters (Heidi Swapp); chipboard accent, rub-ons (K&Co.); acrylic paint; flower (Bazzill); rickrack (May Arts); brad (Making Memories)

the wrecking crew

Alecia Ackerman Grimm
Atlanta, Georgia

Your toddler's childhood friendships play an important role in his or her life, and provide endless memories of laughter, imagination, and—in the case of Alecia's children—mess making! Remember the good times of your child's first friendships on a carefree page. On a layout incorporating numerous photos, layers of circles help establish focal points around the design. Tiny jewelry tags contain captions with little clutter, while label stickers serve as a creative means for journaling. Overlap the title letters on your focal point photo to provide greater impact for the title and a dynamic visual statement.

supplies: Patterned paper, letter stickers (American Crafts); label stickers (Li'l Davis); paper tags (unknown); brads; dye ink; pen; cardstock

73

chapter **four**
daily **life**

✳
✳
✳

From the morning ritual of a favorite cereal and snuggle time on the couch with blankie to the nighttime routine of stories, prayers and bed, life with your toddler may look the same from day to day, but it's guaranteed to never be boring! Treasure the everyday details of these toddler years in your heart and on your scrapbook pages. Record the way your child always wakes you up by singing in her crib, or the way he just can't get enough of Daddy's toolbox. What are his or her favorite pastimes or playgrounds to visit? Celebrate his fascination with the library or the way your little girl loves to try to walk in your high heels. Embrace the sanctity of life and cherish it as the gift it is on pages that highlight the small snapshots that contain big memories from your daily adventures with a toddler.

grocery store

Suzy Plantamura

Laguna Niguel, California

Shopping with a toddler can make your either want to laugh or cry, and oftentimes both, as was the case with Suzy's toddler one chaotic day at the grocery store. Suzy took this photo, capturing the aftermath of her shopping expedition, and journaled the details on curvy, handwritten strips to the left. To achieve the stressed, nerves-on-edge effect of this layout, cut all papers at angles, including your photo. Sweet, cheery colors are a great way to lend irony to your page and enhance the look of innocence in your photo. Suzy used a chipboard arrow to lead from her journaling into the photo, pointing out the story behind the stain on her daughter's shirt. Grocery outings will eventually be done solo once again and these trying times will become sweet memories.

supplies: Velvet paper (SEI); floral ribbon (unknown); chipboard letters (Heidi Swapp, Scenic Route); chipboard arrow (Heidi Swapp); acrylic paint; bubble letters, metal frames (Li'l Davis); markers; pen; cardstock

sweet treat

Tonia Borrosch

Honeoye Falls, New York

A hot day and a toddler with an ice cream cone mean Mom better have her camera ready! Tonia used one enlarged close-up shot of her son testing out his cone, and then used the series of three photos to step through the journaling on this two-page spread. Colorful pattern papers play up the cool and cheery look of ice cream flavors, while a smudge-effect print perfectly illustrates melting ice cream.

supplies: Patterned paper (Scenic Route); rub-ons (Arctic Frog, KI Memories); ribbon (May Arts); eyelets, fabric letter (Making Memories); round tag (Autumn Leaves); paper clips; clear circle accents (unknown); tags (recycled cardboard); thread; Bluecake font (Internet download)

lovin' nanas

Stephanie Barnard
Laguna Niguel, California

Favorite foods go hand-in-hand with favorite ways to eat them, as Stephanie shows on this lighthearted layout displaying her daughter's particularities in eating "nanas." Capture the adorable eating habits of your own toddler utilizing a simple yet lively pattern for the background. Then use a circle punch to create embellishments from the floral-pattern paper and incorporate them throughout the page. Chipboard title letters staggered in a laughing, bouncy arrangement add cheerfulness to the layout.

supplies: Patterned paper, chipboard letters (Scenic Route); circle punch; cardstock; Traditional Print font (Inspire Graphics)

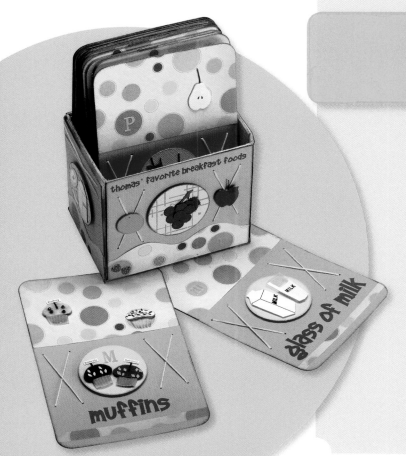

breakfast foods: tags & box

Samuel Cole
Oakdale, Minnesota

Serving as both a clever way to document your child's favorite foods and a learning tool, this unique tag-filled recipe box is a keeper. Thematic stickers are all that are needed to make colorful, simple-shape layouts that allow your child to explore all his favorites in a miniature format. A punched circle with a stitched "X" on either side mimics the look of a table setting while adding a unifying design throughout the set. Coordinate the inside of the box with the outside by using a wave template on coordinating patterned paper and setting it around the exterior of the box.

supplies: Patterned paper (Hot Off The Press); letter stickers (K&Co., Karen Foster); sticker accents (EK Success, Karen Foster, Match'em Ups, Mrs. Grossman's); stamp (Hero Arts); paper floss (Karen Foster); wave cutting template (Creative Memories); circle punch; adhesive foam; corner rounder; pigment ink; cardstock; Poornut font (Internet download)

gravity

Maria Gallardo-Williams
Cary, North Carolina

Many young children wish they could fly and over half of them will attempt it at some point during childhood. Maria created this layout to showcase the large bruise her son received in his failed attempt at flight. A large close-up photo of her son and his fresh bruise fill the page, set on a black and blue background. Hole punches from the patterned papers add a frisky, festive flow about the page, with a single red punch lending a unique, distinct variation in the corner.

supplies: Patterned paper (Club Scrap); rubber stamps (Educational Insights); rub-ons (KI Memories, Scrapworks); dye ink; acrylic paint; hole punch

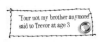

Tonia Borrosch
Honeoye Falls, New York

The adorable sayings of toddlers need a home of their own to be looked at and treasured for years to come. Tonia documented the hilarious gems her son has come up with. A single photo of your child in all his color makes a bold impression against a bright white background, surrounded by his priceless quotes. Machine stitching around the printed transparency quotes set each phrase apart from the background with warmth and definition. Attach a gem brad to embellish each famous saying and add a child-like font for your title.

supplies: Patterned paper (Provo Craft); transparency paper; thread; chipboard heart (Heidi Swapp); brads (Colorbök); cardstock; Evergreen, Jumpstart fonts (Two Peas in a Bucket)

78

3.15 PM

THE DOOR BURSTS OPEN

ENERGY PILES IN

GAKEY! BWADY!

BOUNCE BOUNCE!

JACOB LIFTS ABBY

ON TO THE

TRAMPOLINE.

Bounce

WAY TO MAKE A GIRLS DAY.

bounce bounce

April 2006

bounce bounce

Nic Howard

Pukekohe, New Zealand

What could make your child's day more fun than a romp on the trampoline? Images of your child at play lead to energizing layouts. Use a variety of sizes and textures for title letters, overlapping them and arranging them in waves and curves to mimic the movement in your photos. Arrows and the repetition of title letters set about the page further the jumping joy shown on Nic's design. Short text strips create a lighthearted journaling form, with the spaces between playing up the bouncing effect.

supplies: Patterned paper (Sassafras Lass); chipboard letters (Heidi Swapp); ribbon (Heidi Grace); stamps (Autumn Leaves); dye ink; corner rounder; thread; cardstock; Tasklist font (Two Peas in a Bucket)

Life to a three year old is not always exciting.

Much of the same things day in and day out.

Too many rules and so much just out of your reach.

Boring, ho-hum just another day sort of days.

But there is also so many new things to discover and experience.

The little details of everyday life are exciting and new to you.

Life should not be taken for granted but celebrated each and every day.

It was when I became a mother that I realized what a blessing each day is.

I have opened my eyes and now embrace the daily gift that life is.

Enjoy life and live it colorfully.

Everyday is magical.

Celebrate life!

JUST ANOTHER exciting DAY

another exciting day

Wendy Price

Haddon Twp., New Jersey

Color your child's world with the insight of a mother's wisdom, as Wendy artistically does on this dynamic design. A black-and-white photo is perfect to illustrate the monotony that accompanies a toddler's everyday life, and yet serves as a bold contrast to rich, lively colors used on the remainder of the page on a vast black backdrop. Wendy chose an assortment of cut designs from her scrap papers to come up with her own flower designs, which she transferred onto the cardstock, and then hand-stitched with three-ply floss. Embellish your own creations as Wendy demonstrates, by punching holes from colorful cardstock and adding them to your designs.

supplies: Rub-ons (Scrapworks); circle punches, letter stickers (Making Memories); embroidery floss; pigment ink; cardstock; Century Gothic font (Microsoft)

it's all you

Vicki Boutin
Burlington, Ontario, Canada

Black-and-white images are a perfect means to capture the raw energy of your child's laughter and the intense emotion of joy that comes from a tickle fest. Vicki set her photos against a complementary color scheme of life-affirming green and joy-at-its-finest pink. Frisky and festive ribbons make for bold borders at the top and bottom of the page, and serve as a unifying element in the middle. Create your own unique title embellishments by stamping letters onto chipboard circles and then creating dimension with a diamond glaze.

supplies: Patterned paper (Autumn Leaves, Imagination Project); chipboard letters (BasicGrey, Making Memories); chipboard circles (Bazzill); stamps (Gel-a-tins); pigment ink; brads; ribbon (unknown); dimensional adhesive (Ranger); pen; cardstock

good little monkey

Alecia Ackerman Grimm
Atlanta, Georgia

Bumps and bruises are all part of daily life for a curious toddler. However, some boo-boos require more than a bandage or a kiss from Mom. Alecia records the details here, on this play-by-play page of her son's first trip to the hospital for stitches. Four photos along the left side create a horizontal border that illustrates the story of the stitches, journaled in strips along the right. As Alecia shows here, a favorite character is always a good way to lighten the seriousness of such an unpleasant event. By cutting around a character in the paper to overlap the photo, a touch of cheer is instantly added.

supplies: Patterned paper (American Crafts, Blue Sky); letter stickers (Making Memories); dye ink; cardstock

this look

This look screams "I'm a toddler" with a mind of your own. It means that one minute you're happy as can be and as soon as mommy says "no", you are quick to throw a tantrum. This looks means everything you see or touch is yours and your favorite word is "mine". This look means you love cartoons and dancing to your backyardigans CD. This looks means you are starting to talk and communicate and become the boy you will be. This look screams "I'm a toddler, but not for long".

Marie Cox
Raleigh, North Carolina

Every toddler has at least one look that sums up his very essence in a heartbeat. Marie captured her son's look on this festive page, with journaling to summarize the daily behaviors and short-lived stages that are behind her child's toddler-esque expression in the photo. When you find the image of your own child that captures his personality to a T, be sure to design a page listing the everyday actions—from triumphs to tantrums—in a journaling box that shares the behind-the-scenes details. A page such as this is quick and easy to make. Place cardstock photo corners on a single sheet of patterned paper to serve as border accents and unify the design with the background.

supplies: Patterned paper (Chatterbox); chipboard letters (Creative Imaginations); letter stickers (Making Memories); corner punch; cardstock

quite possibly, probably guilty of something

Tonya Doughty
Wenatchee, Washington

Being ornery is a favorite pastime of toddlers everywhere and is a great subject for a layout. You may have photos of your own toddler where you can't quite remember the incident from the photos, but the image perfectly illustrates a naughty look unique to her. Create a page that smiles at your mischievous toddler's twinkle or impish grin. Tonya kept a solid background to ground the design in dainty pink charm, while employing a bounty of sassy fun flowers and distressed yet dynamic chipboard letters to lend dimensional fun. Chipboard brackets are a great way to pull the eye directionally when a title is spread across the page.

I don't remember exactly what Indy was doing when I took this photo, but I do recall she was up to no good. Even at such a young age →

supplies: Patterned paper, chipboard letters, flowers (Prima); vintage book pages; letter stickers (Die Cuts With A View); quote strips (K&Co.); decorative tape (Target); brads (Queen & Co.); pigment ink; pen; cardstock

82

colour or build LEGO creations, what ever suits your fancy. It is just an ordinary day
On the T.V. we watch Magic School Bus.
a {SLICE} of life
a cup of strawberry milk & a cheese stick
We start each morning with
In the afternoon we have a little lunch and then put the girls down for a nap. Sometimes we
Just an average day.
Hanging out and taking some pictures.
You crawl on to my lap and I hold the camera out in front of us.
SNAP!
A slice of life captured.
Forever, in this priceless photograph.

a slice of life

Vicki Boutin

Burlington, Ontario, Canada

Scrapbooks should be filled not only with the special events of life, but the everyday celebrations of simply being together. Vicki captures a precious memory of afternoons at home with her son, detailing their favorite TV shows to curl up on the couch together to watch and enjoy one another's company. For your own toddler who has too much energy to sit still for picture taking, follow Vicki's example and have your child sit on your lap as you hold the camera out in front of you for a quick shot. Handwritten journaling around the page borders gives aesthetic sentiment to the page, and meshes nicely with personalized black and white pen doodling around the focal point photo.

supplies: Patterned paper (BasicGrey, Mara-Mi); chipboard letter, metal letters (Making Memories); chipboard heart (Heidi Swapp); rub-ons (Autumn Leaves); metal flower (Nunn Design); pigment ink; pen; cardstock; Arial font (Microsoft)

faces of riley

Vicki Boutin
Burlington, Ontario, Canada

Capture the silly side of your child's personality on a powerful yet playful display, such as the one Vicki created using large shapes to form a starburst stage for black-and-white photos. By arranging her images in a row from the main star to the tail behind it, she pulls her two-page spread together in an unbroken flow of movement and style. Coordinating buttons in varying sizes add texture and boyish childhood sentiment to the page. By journaling around complex designs you can incorporate many details of your toddler's inner ham with the heartfelt touch of your own handwriting.

supplies: Patterned paper, chipboard letters (Li'l Davis); letter stamps (Gel-a-tins); pigment ink; buttons (unknown); pen; cardstock

believe

Becky Heisler
Waupaca, Wisconsin

You have the power to encourage your child to reach for her full potential by becoming her greatest cheerleader. Becky gives a bright boost of confidence to her daughter on this lively design, inspired by belief in herself to create a layout using "found" paper. The main background set on an angle is created from the cover of a notebook, with the notebook paper itself serving as the embellished journaling block. Rub-on swirls and circle-dot stamps enhance the look of textural accents, including flowers, buttons and acrylic tiles, while lending a creative energy and visual amusement.

supplies: Pink patterned paper, buttons, rub-on accent (Die Cuts With A View); floral patterned paper (unknown); stamps (Fontwerks, Making Memories); acrylic paint; flowers (Prima); photo corner (Heidi Swapp); acrylic accent tile (KI Memories); brad (Jo-Ann Stores); pen; cardstock

Laura Achilles
Littleton, Colorado

Early on, your child's personality, interests and character traits are well on their way to full bloom. Laura created this sweet, sparkling layout to record her child's distinct self at age three. For a similar look, create an oversized monogram from patterned paper and then list your child's unique likes, loves, hobbies and sayings. A button border along the bottom adds weight and a whimsical touch to the design. Machine stitching in waves about the page give a soft, carefree flow that can be enhanced even further with glitter and glue.

supplies: Patterned paper (Three Bugs in a Rug); buttons (Wal-Mart); ribbon (May Arts); large letter (artist's own design); thread; glitter; pen; cardstock

laugh hysterically when im tickled

want to do whatever sissy is doing

have a very active imagination

love to give and receive big hugs

love to eat snow

have lots of best friends

say every dinner is the bestest in the whole wide world

am caitlyn

am 3 years old

toddler meltdown

Suzy Plantamura
Laguna Niguel, California

When your little sunshine begins to thunder and rain ceaseless tears, look out—a tantrum's on its way. On this clever page design, Suzy incorporated a tantrum flip-book! To achieve this look, cut all papers diagonally and arrange on solid cardstock. Write your journaling between the patterned papers in the empty spaces, and then add rickrack edges for texture and playful motion. Cut white cardstock in circles and fold to open up and reveal additional photos inside. Black-and-white photos allow plenty of freedom in your patterned paper choices, and help convey the sadness and gloom sure to accompany any tantrum.

supplies: Patterned paper (SEI); chipboard letters (Heidi Swapp, Li'l Davis); rickrack (unknown); pen; cardstock

You're two. I get it. You're supposed to have tantrums. You're supposed to think the world revolves around you. You're supposed to want your own way all the time. But boy, you take this to a whole new level! It's not just that you cry. No, you put on a much greater act than that. At the slightest scolding, you crumple to the ground and sob like your heart's been broken. Put you to bed before you're ready and we're guaranteed to hear plaintive wails of "Help me mommy! Help me daddy!" Don't want your diaper changed? Then it's "Ouch!" and "What are you doing?!" as you attempt to wriggle away. Try to keep a hand on you while we cross the street and I get "Stop that!" You are the ultimate 2 year old. But kid, let me tell you, I love you to pieces anyway, my little drama king.

drama king

Barbara Pfeffer
Omaha, Nebraska

Temper tantrums are part of the package when raising your toddler. These moments are definitely worthy of their own scrapbook pages, to look back on in hindsight and see just how far the two of you have come. Barbara chose distressed patterns of red papers to reflect the theme of her child's anger in this two-page spread, and repeated the number "2" throughout to stress her theme. Use your journaling block to record some of the things that your own drama king says when he gets angry.

supplies: Patterned paper (BasicGrey); letter stickers (BasicGrey, K&Co.); brads; AL Old Remington font (Autumn Leaves)

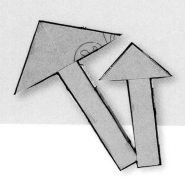

mad chloe mini book

Suzy Plantamura

Laguna Niguel, California

While your toddler's temper may be difficult to deal with in the moment, a mini book showcasing the details of your child's tantrums can provide a source of laughter in hindsight, and a means of coping in the present. A small chipboard album allows for close-up images to capture your child's funny and angry expressions, while rickrack and boisterous patterns convey the sense of explosive emotion. Suzy incorporated actual quotes from her daughter, providing comedic relief and a way to view progress in behavior.

supplies: Chipboard album (Maya Road); patterned paper (unknown); chipboard letters (Heidi Swapp); chipboard hearts (Heidi Grace); large brads, plastic flowers (Queen & Co.); buttons (Buttons Galore); embroidery floss; flower, ribbon (Me & My Big Ideas); rickrack (Doodlebug, Making Memories, Me & My Big Ideas); rhinestones (Making Memories); dye ink; marker; pen; cardstock

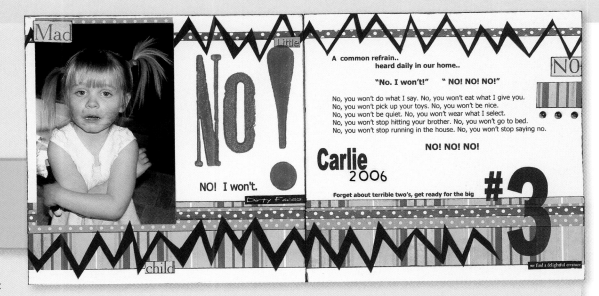

no! i won't!

Dana Swords

Doswell, Virginia

What parent can't relate to the scenario illustrated on Dana's two-page layout: the disgruntled child, with hair a mess and attitude in a determined knot? A little humor is a great way to cope with your child's difficult stages. A page such as this is a great place to vent a little through journaling, let go through jagged edges and loud colors, and laugh a little through classic photos that capture the humor of your child's stubborn episodes. Large letter stamps in bold and boisterous colors are perfect for making a pronounced statement a little louder.

supplies: Patterned paper (Anna Griffin, Bo-Bunny, Die Cuts With A View, K&Co., My Mind's Eye); foam stamps (Li'l Davis, Making Memories); acrylic paint; dye ink; cardstock; Arial, Tahoma fonts (Microsoft)

Maria Gallardo-Williams
Cary, North Carolina

Since many toddlers think of hair cuts as a form of brutal torture, home hair cuts seem to be the best option. On this calm and collected page design, Maria journals the sweat and tears that go into cutting her son's hair at home. Use a clear, bold shot of your child after the process to top off your journaling block, and accentuate the image with colorful photo corners. A ribbon-framed accent photo lends texture and a festive element to your layout. Rolled, chalked edges on background papers keep your design from appearing too polished, and convey the sense of struggle endured by most parents when attempting the role of hair stylist.

supplies: Patterned paper (Laura Ashley, SEI); epoxy letters (Doodlebug); ribbon (Offray); embroidery floss; photo corners; chalk; cardstock; Batik font (Internet download)

so happy

Courtney Walsh
Winnebago, Illinois

Watching your toddler explore the great outdoors is cause for everyday celebration, as Courtney attests on this joyful page design showcasing her son in his treehouse. Energetic colors and patterns express the excitement and enthusiasm of a child's bliss, while patterned chipboard letters draw the eye inward to the photo. By arranging papers and photo into a rectangle on a dark blue background, Courtney achieved the look of a treehouse, reflected in the photo. Velvety rub-on letters enhance the warm, fuzzy feeling of the page, with letter stickers and white pen used to complete the title.

supplies: Patterned paper (KI Memories, Scenic Route); chipboard accents, letter stickers (KI Memories); ribbon (Chatterbox); fuzzy rub-ons (Heidi Swapp); staples; file stickers; pen; cardstock

little things

Kim Moreno
Tucson, Arizona

A simple way to bring new life to shadowy photos is to play up the emotion of the images on a lively layout. Using a mixture of bright colors and energetic patterns, Kim captured the excitement of her son discovering a ladybug. Setting accent photos inside chipboard brackets provides an interesting way to provide definition for small images, especially those overlapping larger photos. To zoom in on a tiny detail in your photos, such as the ladybug, use a circular silhouette rub-on around the point of focus. Kim stamped layered circles of dots around the silhouette to enhance the look.

supplies: Patterned paper (American Crafts); chipboard accents (Everlasting Keepsakes); brads, rub-ons (Making Memories); stamps (Fontwerks, Sassafras Lass); stamping ink; journaling accents, photo corner (Heidi Swapp); circle punch; pen; cardstock

89

bully

ANT

Poor little bugs.
Jakai doesnt mean to squish you in the midst of his excitement at catching one of you. He just thinks you are so cool. I know its not fun being trapped underneath one of his sandals but hes just testing how fast you are. i try and tell him to leave you guys alone, but he just loves bugs.

ant bully

Marie Cox

Raleigh, North Carolina

Your child's fascination with the world of bugs makes for rich layouts filled with the wonder of all creatures great and small. Undistracted backgrounds immediately allow a viewer to zoom in on your focal point photo, and with help from an arrow the eye instantly picks out the details in your photo. Thematic rub-ons, such as the insects at the base of Marie's journaling box, are a simple way to balance out a page while adding visual excitement. When using minimal embellishment on your creations, arrange the photo, title and journaling box in staggered style and use a small decorative paper band for unifying balance and support.

supplies: Patterned paper (Provo Craft); chipboard letters (Creative Imaginations); letter stickers (Doodlebug); rub-ons (Making Memories); cardstock

Tonia Borrosch
Honeoye Falls, New York

Sometimes life lessons serve a dual purpose to teach both child and parent. Tonia's page of wisdom reminds us to never blink for a second when a toddler has rocks and the side of a car for a canvas in sight! To highlight a journaled photo detail, use strips of patterned paper with an embellished triangle at the tip to form arrows. The arrows create movement and a flow of vision as well as color and insight. Scalloped paper borders balance out a layout composed mainly of sleek lines, while colorful buttons set inside the rounded edges give whimsical dimension.

supplies: Patterned paper (KI Memories, Provo Craft, Scenic Route); scalloped cardstock (Bazzill); letter and number stickers (American Crafts); brads; buttons (Chatterbox); accent sticker (7 Gypsies); pen; cardstock

prize fighter

Alecia Ackerman Grimm
Atlanta, Georgia

If your child's birthday photos seem to always showcase a major bump or bruise, consider creating an injury story layout. Share the details of a major boo-boo and the events surrounding it. For a dynamic title that serves as a stand-alone page element, paint over mask letters with a foam brush. Then remove the mask to reveal the background beneath within the outlines. Use the same paint with a decorative stamp to balance out the title, and then repeat the decorative image with black pen throughout the page.

supplies: Patterned paper (Adorn It); foam stamp, letter mask (Heidi Swapp); ledger paper (unknown); acrylic paint; brads; pigment ink; pen; cardstock

91

Kelly Goree
Shelbyville, Kentucky

Your child in his element makes for fun-filled scrapbook pages. In this layout, Kelly showcases her son's two favorites: chalk and the great outdoors. Create a variety of star templates to make patterned paper accents. Use an oversized star or other shape to frame your focal point photo. Add movement and texture by hand-stitching whimsical embellishments to your page. Distressed pattern papers and soft colors capture the effect of chalk and provide a contrasting backdrop for bold chipboard letters.

supplies: Patterned paper, chipboard shapes, letter stickers (BasicGrey); chipboard letters (Heidi Swapp); pigment ink; embroidery floss; pen; cardstock

lite brite

Kim Moreno
Tucson, Arizona

The intensity of a child focusing on a new activity or classic toy is enough to light up any page. Use colors and patterns to emphasize the activity of the photos, such as the polka-dot patterns and large, colorful brads Kim used on her layout. To make a page element similar to the title box in the lower right, punch holes in black background paper, placing colored paper behind it. Layer glossy embellishments over each punched hole and allow the colors to shine through.

supplies: Patterned paper (CherryArte); chipboard letters (Creative Imaginations); chipboard accent (Pressed Petals); brads; glossy accents (Ranger); vellum adhesive paper (Therm O Web); pen; cardstock

play doh days

Alecia Ackerman Grimm
Atlanta, Georgia

Rainy days call for a little imagination and a lot of Play Doh. To incorporate lots of photos onto one layout, fill an entire page completely with images. To provide captions for each image, number each photo with a rub-on and give the details on a corresponding thought bubble sticker. Rub-on stitches are a simple way to add fun and create a unifying effect throughout the layout.

supplies: Patterned paper (American Crafts, Scrapworks, SEI); letter stickers (American Crafts, SEI); bubble stickers (SEI); rub-on accents (Doodlebug, Making Memories); dye ink; pen; cardstock

Tonia Borrosch
Honeoye Falls, New York

Disciplining your children is never easy, especially with such angelic faces on such boundary-pushing bodies. Tonia's journaling illustrates the difficult necessity of "tough love." A patterned background can be easily created using a large rubber stamp to fill in empty blocks. Playful embellishments were created at the top with a metal-rimmed circle tag, accentuated with a screw eyelet and an acrylic heart to illustrate the stamped words inside.

supplies: Patterned paper (Westrim); acrylic heart, letter stickers (Creative Imaginations); rubber stamp (Close to My Heart); dye ink; ribbon (Offray); letter stamps (PSX); eyelets; circle tag (Impress Rubber Stamps); number accent (Deluxe Designs); cardstock

routine chart

Leah Blanco Williams
Rochester, New York

A magnetic routine chart is a simple way to give children a sense of security and responsibility and parents a sense of structure and peace. With a magnetic dry erase board as the background, Leah used cardstock to frame her patterned paper focus, and added acrylic star jewels and wooden train accents for additional fun.

supplies: Magnetic dry-erase board (Board Dudes); patterned paper (K&Co.); ribbon (Jo-Ann Stores, Offray); wooden train (Darice); button, wooden letter, star jewels (unknown); acrylic paint; circle punch; dye ink; embroidery floss; glitter glue; magnet; cardstock; Amazone font (Bitstream); Smilage font (ScrapVillage)

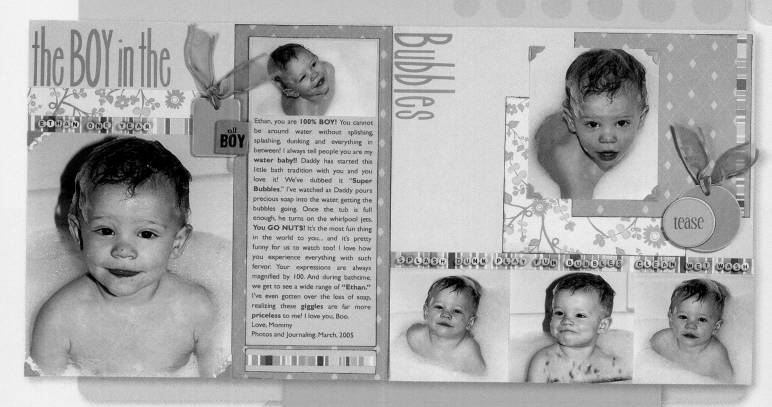

the b°y in the bubbles

Courtney Walsh
Winnebago, Illinois

The priceless expressions of your child experiencing the simple joys of life, such as a bubble bath, are huge reminders to stop and sense the world through a child's eyes. Utilizing a complementary orange and blue color scheme captures the sheer exuberance of Courtney's son in the bubbles, and plays up the blue water while adding masculine flair. Letter bead words lend a childlike look and enhance the bath time theme of the page.

supplies: Letter stickers, patterned paper, photo corners, word sticker, wooden tags (Chatterbox); ribbon (Offray); pigment ink; letter beads (unknown); cardstock; Arial font (Microsoft)

A true story by Josiah (me!)

EXPLORE. WONDER. PLAY. BE. INDEPENDEN

CURIOUS. LAUGH. CUDDLE. EXCITEMENT. CURIOSITY. AMAZING. CU

t u b b i e s   r

me

mommy fills the big tub just for me. I fill my boat. I dump it out. (Repeat 100 times.) I laugh. I play. I pucker up just for momma! Yep. I love tubbies!

tubbies-r-me

Sharon Laakkonen
Superior, Wisconsin

Bathtime can be a child's favorite time of the day, perfect for splashing, exploring, pouring and dumping. A circular theme is a great way to elicit the look of bubbles and water splashes, and create a carefree vibe of freewheeling fun. Sharon trimmed her patterned paper in varying sizes of circles for added enthusiasm and energetic bounce. Colorful title brads and machine stitching further the theme and add texture and style.

supplies: Patterned paper (Imagination Project); circle accents, decorative strips (Provo Craft); letter brads (Queen & Co.); solvent ink; thread; pen; cardstock

bedtime routine

Greta Hammond

Goshen, Indiana

Your child's bedtime routine is something to be treasured long after the Pooh-bear nightlight is packed away. A stark black background serves the dual purpose of providing bold contrast while establishing a nighttime appearance. The use of spirals and circle-patterned art tape elicit a sleepytime effect, enhanced with soft floral notions, overlapping and tucked behind photos and title letters. Greta used black-and-white accent photos to illustrate several portions of her daughter's bedtime rituals and add to the dreamy look of the page.

supplies: Patterned paper, decorative art tape, coaster letters and accents, rub-ons (Imagination Project); brads; cardstock

97

prelude to dreamland

Leora Sanford
Pocatella, Idaho

Cherished lullabyes create sleepy, soft sentimental pages, when added as text to your toddler's layouts. Capture this dynamic look on your own creations by composing your design with image-editing software, printing it off and adding the actual photo to the page. A black-and-white photo adds to the bedtime beauty of the theme, while a strong composition of title and favorite nighttime songs balances out the bottom.

supplies: Cardstock; digital flower, journaling box, punctuation (Designer Digitals); Century Gothic font (Microsoft); Susie's Hand font (Internet download)

nite-nite

Kim Moreno
Tucson, Arizona

Wrap up your child's bedtime rituals in a warm, cozy page like Kim's dreamy design featuring her son with his blanket and paci. A decorative chipboard border is covered in patterned paper to mimic the snuggly look of a blankie; a satin ribbon accent at the top coordinates with the photo. Velvety letter stickers convey the soft warmth of bedtime blankets, while inked edges lend a soothing dreamland glow of definition.

supplies: Patterned paper (Three Bugs in a Rug); chipboard accent (Magistical Memories); pigment ink; brads; letter stickers (Heidi Swapp); decorative punch (EK Success); ribbon (unknown); pen; cardstock; A Little Pot font (Internet download)

treasure (trezh′er) 1. accumulated wealth 2. something of great worth 3. irreplaceable, priceless

enduring (en·door′in) 1. lasting, permanent 2. continuing on until the end

Drews

prayer

Dear Heavenly Father
Thank you this day,
Thank you for the food,
Thank you for Mommy,
And Daddy,
And Binnie,
And Mommy and Daddy,
Bless the seatbelts
so we can be safe,
In the name Jesus Christ,
AMEN

drew's prayer

Amy Farnsworth

Brighton, Colorado

How precious the sound of your child's first prayers. Remember them always on a serene and sentimental layout, using journaling strips to record the favorite heartfelt prayers your child lifts up. A black-and-white focal point photo evokes quiet emotion. The sepia tone, transparent smaller images are created using a ghost embossing technique. The technique involves a text weight paper, two coats of melted UTEE, and heating the photos until the UTEE seeps through here and there.

supplies: Patterned paper (7 Gypsies, Crate Paper); chipboard letters and shapes (Li'l Davis); plastic letters (Heidi Swapp); button (Bazzill); ribbon (May Arts); word stickers (Making Memories); metal charm (Pebbles); stamp (Dream Street); dye ink; fabric (unknown); thread; Attic font (Internet download)

chapter five
adventures
in the world

Every day with a toddler could qualify as an adventure to most parents, but special explorations need special pages to celebrate the thrills and wonders life has to offer. First trips to the zoo or the ocean are memories sure to imprint their signature on your heart. Whether your toddler's travels lead him half way across the world or to adventures in his own back yard, take part in exploring life through the innocence and awe of your child's eyes. Take time to dig in the dirt with your tot and see just how far a hole can go. Ride the carousel with your little girl to react to the way colors and movement combine with music in a wonderful, whirling dance. As your child's adventures lure him from the living room, be sure to create scrapbook pages to always keep the thrill of these explorations just a photo album away.

Christine Traversa
Joliet, Illinois

A child's expression can convey appreciation for the wonders of the universe and the thrill of simply being alive. Have a camera ready when your child takes on new challenges and experiences for the first time, discovering new ways to use her amazing body. Expressions such as these are priceless reminders to always keep a sense of wonder and celebrate the joy of living. Capture the look of authentic bliss on your own creations through lively colors and playful prints with just a handful of thematic stickers added for fun.

supplies: Patterned paper, stickers (Provo Craft); adhesive foam; image editing software (Adobe); cardstock

discover summer

Greta Hammond
Goshen, Indiana

A few strips of descriptive phrases were all that were needed to add a finishing touch to a charming tribute to her toddler's puddle-play discoveries. Use a circle cutter to create a large patterned paper loop, which can be set behind portions of your focal-point photo to emphasize details in your image. Photos taken from different viewpoints add interest and help to recreate the memory from varying vantage points. Greta used black pen to add a cohesive design of dots around her cut circles and throughout her minimal embellishments.

supplies: Patterned paper (My Mind's Eye); chipboard letters (Heidi Swapp); rub-on letters (Making Memories); rub-on flowers (Autumn Leaves); chipboard flower (Bazzill); acrylic paint; brads, photo corners (Chatterbox); dye ink; pen; Times New Roman font (Microsoft)

102

dirty diva

Amy Farnsworth

Brighton, Colorado

Even the girliest of "girly-girls" can't resist a little fun in the dirt once in awhile. For pages that feature ironic situations with your little princess, ribbons and rhinestones and floral prints are always a hit providing endless creative possibilities. Amy wove her ribbons into a crown-like pattern at the top of her page, embellishing her die-cut flowers with glimmering gems. Rhinestones were also used to embellish her title letters. A decorative label holder is perfect for zooming in on details in your photos, as Amy demonstrates with the highlighted look at her daughter's hands.

supplies: Patterned paper, title letters (Three Bugs in a Rug); flowers, flower rhinestones (Heidi Swapp); rhinestones (Darice); large bookplate (BasicGrey); small bookplate (Making Memories); letter stickers (KI Memories); puff paint; ribbon (May Arts); transparency; Century Gothic font (Microsoft)

sunshine

Marie Cox
Raleigh, North Carolina

Capture the thrill of your child's first trip to the ocean on a warm, sunny page. By using a decorative border in a sultry shade, the look and feel of summer sun helps your layout glow in thematic style. A single patterned paper block set beneath your focal image accentuates the fun-filled emotion of a day at the beach, and can be balanced by a punched photo corner from the same design.

supplies: Patterned paper (Sassafras Lass); die-cut cardstock (Bazzill); number stickers (Making Memories); photo corner punch; rub-ons (unknown); cardstock

meet me in hawaii, thomas

Samuel Cole
Woodsbury, Minnesota

Vacation takes on a whole new meaning when you travel with a child. Forget lounging on the beach—there are sandcastles to be built! When designing your own beach-themed page, a wave cutter lends the perfect effect to a tropical tribute. Using thematic patterned papers, rub-ons and stickers will add to the fun. A circle cutter can be used to highlight specific features in your photos or to create a playful overlapping element.

supplies: Patterned paper, rub-ons, stickers (Karen Foster); circle punch; circle cutter; wave cutter (Creative Imaginations); pen; cardstock

104

day of fishing
crater lake
june 2001

fun wall decoration

Laura Achilles

Littleton, Colorado

A wall swag is an eye-pleasing way to remind your family of the joy of a special day. Showcase photos from the event and display heartfelt journaling. To design your own word-themed creation, purchase pre-made letters from your local craft store and cover in a patterned paper that reinforces the emotion of the word or event. Use floral wire to tie various ribbons and fabric strips in a variety of widths and lengths. Drill small holes near the bottom of each letter and attach floral wire into the holes. To hang your photos, make sure that some ribbons are slightly longer than others, and attach bulldog clips to hold images and journaling in place.

supplies: Wooden letters (Provo Craft); patterned paper (BasicGrey); clips (Making Memories); flowers (Heidi Swapp, Petaloo); ribbon (May Arts, Offray); wire; button; pen

freedom

Shannon Taylor
Bristol, Tennessee

Oh, to know the world as freely as a toddler—free of worries and inhibitions. Shannon embraced these moments of innocence, on a layout featuring her nephew running buck naked through the clover. Rub-on flourishes set vertically float the eye up and beyond the layout boundaries. To include extensive journaling on a layout, yet still have the photos stand alone, attach a matted photo element to the page with jumprings, allowing the large portion of the page to lift and reveal hidden journaling.

supplies: Patterned paper, fibers, metal accents (BasicGrey); letter stickers (Mustard Moon); buttons (Making Memories); jump rings (Junkitz); thread; Jayne Print font (Internet download)

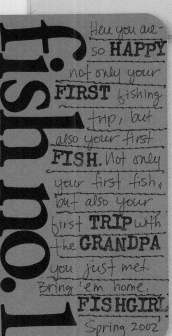

Tonya Doughty
Wenatchee, Washington

Your child's first fishing trip is a momentous event. Layering multiple mats around your focal-point photo creates a visually appealing frame, while drawing the eye in, as if to a bull's-eye. Tonya underlined her journaling with red stitching for texture and coordinating color. To balance the weight of the page, use black ink to stamp words you wish to emphasize and large black letter stickers for the title.

supplies: Patterned paper (Die Cuts With A View); ribbon (Offray); letter stickers (American Crafts); letter stamps (EK Success); pigment ink; thread; pen; cardstock

down on the farm

Vicki Boutin
Burlington, Ontario, Canada

To capture the excitement found in a trip to the zoo, wildlife expedition or petting farm, a bouncy arrangement of free-wheeling patterns on cut paper circles lends an effervescent energy to any layout. Varying sizes and colors of brads surrounding several cut circles add to the visual fun. Vicki mounted her focal-point image on a puffy paper and chipboard tiles for a 3-D effect, and added a high-spirited accent created with wire and beads.

supplies: Patterned paper (We R Memory Keepers); letter stickers (American Crafts); rub-on letter (Imagination Project); labels (Dymo); chipboard shapes (Bazzill); brads (Making Memories, Queen & Co.); charms (Nunn Designs); beads, wire (unknown); adhesive foam; circle cutter; cardstock

A Day in the Park

and Christy

TWO SISTERS

love to laugh

and play together

at the park.

They always have a blast!

June 2006

a day in the park

Amanda Williams

Tucson, Arizona

A tiny book just your toddler's size holds memories the whole family will enjoy looking through again and again. Amanda designed this mini album to record a typical day of her girls enjoying the great outdoors. She used cheerful, sunny papers and simple-shape embellishments to make this album kid-friendly. Children love to look at photographs of themselves, and when displayed in an inviting album just the right size for their hands, they can relive their daily adventures with just a flip of the page.

supplies: Accordion album, patterned paper, fabric thread, metal embellishments, ribbon (American Traditional); plastic ring (Junkitz); safety pin (Making Memories); flower (Heidi Swapp); button; brad; dye ink; cardstock

DETERMINE to BE TENDER with THE YOUNG

COMPASSIONATE With The ELDERLY

SYMPATHETIC To Those who struggle

and TOLERANT With The Weak & Wrong

BECAUSE at some POINT in Your LIFE YOU WILL HAVE BEEN ALL of THESE

GeoRge W CarVer

compassion

Kathy Fesmire
Athens, Tennessee

Sometimes greeting cards can serve as the perfect inspiration for heartfelt journaling, as Kathy shows on her layout expressing the compassion conveyed on her son's face during a zoo expedition. A vibrant color set behind a black-and-white image pulls the eye to the photo, when set against a stark white background with simple accents. Kathy split her journaling quote and separated the lines with individual color blocks for emphasis.

supplies: Patterned paper, letter stamps, letter stickers, ribbon, rub-ons, sticker accents (EK Success); ink; cardstock

When you were two, we went to New Orleans for Spring Break. We visited the Audubon Zoo and saw the animals, fed the ducks and watched the sea lions perform. We stopped at the playground and let you ride the carousel. This was your first "real" carousel ride! Dad went with you so I wouldn't get dizzy and, of course, I wanted to take photos of you.

carousel

Melanie Douthit
West Monroe, Louisiana

The thrill of a first carousel ride is a memorable feeling not only for a child but for parents there to experience the sensation once again. Melanie recounts her child's carousel debut on this classic childhood layout. For the vintage look of weathered wood, use chipboard letters painted with metallic paint. Transfer the look of lights circling the ride and the intricately painted ponies by using white bead paint to add dotted "light" accents and detailed doodling. Convey the sensation of movement on your page by adding wavy stitched accents and buttons.

supplies: Patterned paper (Flair Designs, Scenic Route); chipboard letters (Everlasting Keepsakes); chipboard flower (Bazzill); stickers (Flair Designs); buttons (unknown); metallic paint; dimensional paint; pigment ink; thread; cardstock

the world's music

Natalie Bensimhon
Easton, Pennsylvania

A child's exploration of the world of music inspires parents to document these delightful discoveries in design. A poem appropriate to your photo can create a beautiful visual masterpiece, with no further journaling required. Natalie pulled elements from the poem, such as the flowers cut from patterned paper and a freeform bird accent made with a combination of paisley patterned paper and her own designs. Hand-drawn doodles flow from her photo and unify the embellishments into a symphony for the eyes.

supplies: Patterned paper (SEI); pen; Kraft cardstock

isaac picture frame

Kathy Fesmire
Athens, Tennessee

Adventures in eating are fun memories to frame in clever creations. To incorporate the look of the orient in your own framed creations, cover a frame with pieces of a bamboo placemat, trimmed to fit. To make her own bamboo accents, Kathy wrapped strips of green paper around several wooden sticks pulled from her placemat and then added wire-framed leaves. An Asian-themed stamp can spruce up a title or embellishment, such as a folded napkin, while chopsticks lend a finishing touch.

supplies: Frame (EK Success); wooden circles and letters (Plaid); chopsticks, placemat, stamp (unknown); dye ink; acrylic paint; decoupage medium; cardstock

screaming on a jet plane

Erin Campbell-Pope
Petal, Mississippi

Just when you thought it was safe to soar the friendly skies, the pilot turns off the "fasten your seat-belt" sign. These and other parental tortures of traveling with a toddler can attain comedic value in hindsight, when made into a lighthearted layout. An airplane die-cut, angled inward on a two-page spread pulls the eye into the design and establishes a unique visual arrangement for journaling beneath. Incorporate collected ephemera from your trip, such as plane tickets and luggage tags, and add handwritten captions for fun. Erin used humorous, tongue-in-cheek journaling to take one emotionally turbulent plane ride and turn it into a difficult, but funny memory.

supplies: Patterned paper, ribbon (American Crafts); chipboard letters (Heidi Swapp); chipboard accents (Chatterbox); acrylic paint; rub-ons (Making Memories); die-cut airplane (Deluxe Designs); stickers (7 Gypsies); circle punch; thread; airplane ticket; authentic luggage stickers; cardstock

hawaii vacation mini album

Suzy Plantamura
Laguna Niguel, California

Remember your toddler's adventures on a family vacation with a fun and festive mini album. Use patterned papers appropriate to your travel destination. Let your imagination run wild in the minimized space, arranging your images in a variety of shapes and positions for visual excitement. Choose a single embellishment or signature look for unity, such as the circles Suzy incorporated onto each of her layouts, and the handwritten journaling throughout.

supplies: Patterned paper, metal accent, printed titles, stickers, tags (Wal-Mart); fabric, ribbon (unknown); brads (Bazzill, SEI); flower (Prima); acrylic paint; dye ink; marker; pen; cardstock

disney lunch box book

Kathy Fesmire
Athens, Tennessee

Pack away the photo fun of a family trip in a thematic lunch box. Simple embellishments of 3-D stickers coordinating with your trip's theme are an easy way to adorn your mini book holder. Add a title to the outside and colorful buttons to finish the look. Bold and beautiful ribbons tied to the lunch box handle add texture. Kathy's mini book was quick and easy to make. She bound cardstock with a ribbon to hold 3½" x 5" photos of her child with various characters from the numerous Disney theme parks.

supplies: Mini lunch box (Target); accent and letter stickers (EK Success); ribbons (American Crafts, Offray); buttons (unknown); cardstock

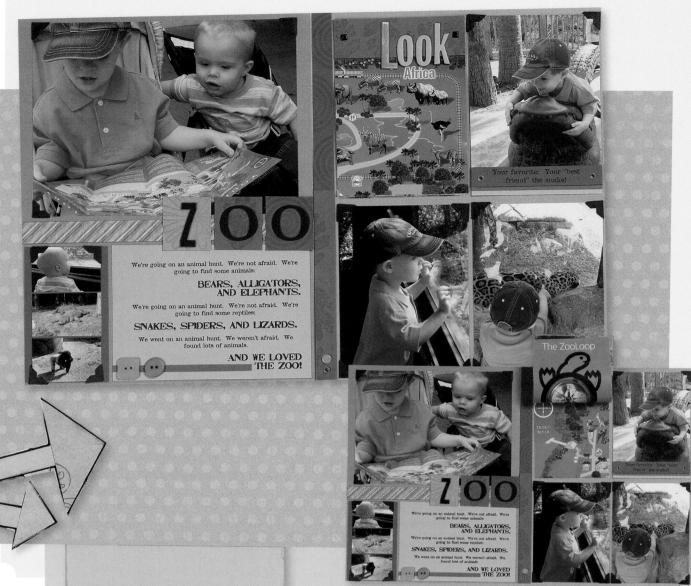

ZOO

Jennifer Gallacher
American Fork, Utah

Safari adventures can be lots of fun when experienced from the comfort of a stroller. For all your wild zoo expeditions, consider cutting squares from the actual zoo map and incorporating them into your design. Jennifer attached her map squares to the layout with mini brads, so the squares flip up to show more map mementos. For a graphic edge, add concentric circle and leaf stamp imprints with watermark ink throughout.

supplies: Cardstock; stamps (EK Success, Fontwerks, Hero Arts); watermark ink; brads, chipboard letters, eyelets, snaps (Making Memories); buttons (Making Memories, SEI); photo corners; ribbon (unknown); Antique Type font (ScrapVillage)

stuck

Kathy Fesmire

Athens, Tennessee

Even the messiest moments of life with your toddler are memories to laugh about in years to come. To help remember the details of your own child's delight in all things slimy, dirty, mucky and/or muddy, follow Kathy's journalistic style. On this two-page spread, she neatly arranged and numbered her photos to correspond with numbered journaling hidden beneath the row of images on the left-hand page. To re-create the look of mud or grime on your layouts, smear a mixture of artist cement and paint around your design.

supplies: Patterned paper (Chatterbox, Karen Foster, Pebbles, Provo Craft); letter stickers (Chatterbox, EK Success, Pebbles); tag stickers (Pebbles); ribbon (Offray); number stickers (KI Memories); letter stamps (Making Memories, Plaid); date stamp, foam stamps, rub-ons (Making Memories); acrylic paint; ink; artist's cement (USArtQuest); brads; hinges (unknown)

One of the best things about Nicholas is his good disposition. Whenever Victoria has a horse show, he willingly comes along and finds a way to entertain himself.

On this chilly day at Southern Oaks, he spend a lot of time playing around the fields, looking for deer tracks and inspecting all the big trees on the property. As you can see, he even had to hug some of them!

tree hugger

Maria Gallardo-Williams
Cary, North Carolina

Celebrate nature's artistry on visually rich layouts, such as Maria's showing her son's fascination with the great outdoors. With photos where eye-pleasing textures are in high definition, such as in the tree bark or leaves, little else is needed on your page. Use subtle patterns in subdued tones to allow the beauty of creation to burst forth from your photos in its own rich designs. Maria used small snippets of complementary papers to allow the tree to shine for itself, along with her little tree hugger.

supplies: Patterned paper (Bo-Bunny, Karen Foster); letter stickers, ribbon (Doodlebug); dye ink; circle punch; pen; cardstock

weary traveler

Tonia Borrosch
Honeoye Falls, New York

While traveling can be hard on just about anyone, a busy itinerary is always hardest on our children. When your tot has reached his limit, a few photos can illustrate the emotion of a stressful journey. Incorporate your child's plane ticket onto the page design and embellish the ticket with stapled ribbons for texture and fun. Balance the look by stitching a thematic pocket, embellish with a luggage sticker, and tuck details of a jam-packed journey inside on a tag adorned with ribbons.

supplies: Patterned paper (Rusty Pickle); ribbon (May Arts, Offray); foam stamps (Making Memories); acrylic paint; tags (office supply store); rub-ons (Chatterbox); transparency; travel sticker (Melissa Frances); airline ticket; thread; staples; dye ink; pen

frisbee fun

Amy Farnsworth

Brighton, Colorado

To play up the theme of a favorite summer pastime, such as Frisbee throwing, incorporate a large circle for your background. Amy added a colorful chipboard arrow inside a smaller circle outline to draw attention to the miniscule flying Frisbee in the distance of her black-and-white accent shot. To mimic the layered look in the title letters, stamp your title onto a transparency, cut out the individual letters and overlap them on the page.

supplies: Patterned paper (BasicGrey); chipboard letters (Pressed Petals); chipboard accents (BasicGrey, Heidi Swapp, KI Memories); metal accents (BasicGrey, Making Memories); letter stamps (Magnetic Poetry); acrylic paint; label maker (Dymo); circle cutter; cardstock; Century Gothic font (Microsoft)

cool compromise

Jennifer Gallacher
American Fork, Utah

A blue and yellow color scheme is perfect for expressing a cool jaunt through a sprinkler on a hot summer day, while black matting around the images plays up her son's sense of injustice. For a fair and balanced account of those head-butting incidents, such as wearing a T-shirt, use the he-thought/she-thought format shown here. Jennifer used her sheet of colorful letter stickers as inspiration for the layout and then designed the spread around the grid.

supplies: Patterned paper (Target); letter and accent stickers (Creative Imaginations, Pebbles); chipboard stars (Heidi Swapp); brads; cardstock; SP You've Got Mail font (Scrapsupply)

new sheriff

Greta Hammond
Goshen, Indiana

Greta chose the theme for this stellar creation based on her daughter's sheriff duds. A handful of tiny accent images will nestle neatly around an overall shot of your own child's outfit in a focal-point photo. A single thematic embellishment, such as the sheriff's star, can be layered and repeated to play up the fun. Greta added concentric circle stamps over her title letters to contrast with the sharp, clean edges of the stars.

supplies: Patterned paper, coaster letters and shapes, rub-ons (Imagination Project); circles stamp (Hero Arts); pigment ink; pen; cardstock; Times New Roman font (Microsoft)

the reluctant dragon

Vicki Boutin
Burlington, Ontario, Canada

Even those difficult toddler times, such as when your little one gets impatient having his photo taken, are worth the effort in scrapping the whole adventure of life. Vicki used one great shot of her son in Halloween gear as her focal-point image and then set a row of images along the bottom to show the true confessions of a toddler's attention span. A small photo in the middle, with cut slits for a brad-studded strip to run through, serves as a visual illustration of the abrupt drop in the emotion of this photo session on this playful page.

supplies: Patterned paper, letter stickers (Heidi Grace); stamp (Gel-a-tins); dye ink; brads; metal tag (unknown); label (Dymo); pen; cardstock

Greta Hammond
Goshen, Indiana

The thrill of your child's first trick-or-treat experience deserves a delightful design. Highlight your child's favorite part of the festivities as the theme for your own layout, using a handful of embellishments to play up the fun in the photos. Greta used an all black background with vibrant inked title letters and corresponding orange buttons to further the Halloween theme and coordinate with her daughter's costume.

supplies: Patterned paper, coaster letters (Imagination Project); rub-on letters and accent (Autumn Leaves); chipboard star (BasicGrey); buttons (unknown); pen; cardstock; Times New Roman font (Microsoft)

halloween costumes

Courtney Walsh
Winnebago, Illinois

When a traditional black and orange color scheme won't do for your favorite Halloween photos, play up the colors of your children's costumes instead. Utilize a few large blocks of coordinating patterned papers with cardstock strips along the top and bottom of the page. A trio of brads set at opposing corners of the layout balance the weight of the creation, while a distressed wooden frame in a matching color embraces the basic facts of your page in style.

supplies: Patterned paper, book cloth, letter stickers, photo corners, wood frame (Chatterbox); ribbon (Offray); brads; pigment ink; cardstock; Times New Roman font (Microsoft)

i eat snow

Greta Hammond

Goshen, Indiana

Adventures in the wintry outdoors may result in a fabulous edible find—snow! A couple of expressive photos can illustrate a humorous story behind the images on your page. Greta used her daughter's comical quote as the title for her layout, drawing the viewer directly into the journaling for the details. To create a wet, icy look on your own designs, coat chipboard letters and flower accents with a glossy medium. Inked edges around title letters also help emphasize a smeared, wet, snowy look.

supplies: Patterned paper, coaster letters, flowers, rub-ons (Imagination Project); pigment ink; glossy accents (Ranger); hole punch; thread; cardstock; Times New Roman font (Microsoft)

love that hat

Vicki Boutin
Burlington, Ontario, Canada

Great winter weather adventures call for a great winter hat and a great winter-themed layout to celebrate them both. A chilly blue background sets a cool tone on any snowbound page, while snow-flake-themed papers add to the drama. Vicki took photos of her own little snow-bunny in an adorable, oversized hat. For a hint of cold weather glitz, iridescent glitter set around dimensional elements, such as the chipboard heart, gives a frosty look and adds textural charm.

supplies: Patterned paper, chipboard letters (Scenic Route); chipboard heart (Imagination Project); metal flower (Karen Foster); heart brads (unknown); acrylic paint; iridescent glitter; sandpaper; marker; pen; cardstock

let's call him chuck

Courtney Walsh
Winnebago, Illinois

Your child's first snowman-making endeavors are memories to treasure. Courtney celebrates the hilarity of her daughter's first snowman friend on this chilly, silly winter-fun page. Circles cut from patterned papers play up the theme of the page, while rotating cool-colored buttons enhance the snowball effect. Three large patterned paper circles in the background establish a visual triangle.

supplies: Patterned paper (Autumn Leaves, Mustard Moon); letter stickers (Chatterbox); rub-ons (KI Memories); buttons (Junkitz); embroidery floss; cardstock

parade

Erin Campbell-Pope
Petal, Mississippi

Who doesn't love a parade? To see a parade through the eyes of a child is an experience guaranteed to make your heart smile. The use of color, repetition of shapes, and well-placed lines march the viewer's eyes about the page. A simple memento from the parade can serve as the inspiration for choosing your page elements. Erin used silver, inspired by the jingle bell her daughter received, and added silver leafing to her title letters and metal trim to the borders.

supplies: Patterned paper, file tabs (SEI); chipboard letters, metal trim (Making Memories); definition coaster (My Mind's Eye); rub-ons (Making Memories, Royal & Langnickel); bell sticker (Creative Imaginations); ribbon (American Crafts, Offray); lace (unknown); dye ink; circle cutter; hole punch; thread; silver leafing pen; pen; cardstock

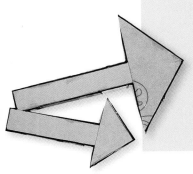

source guide

The following companies manufacture products featured in this book. Please check your local retailers to find these materials, or go to a company's Web site for the latest product. In addition, we have made every attempt to properly credit the items mentioned in this book. We apologize to any company that we have listed incorrectly, and would appreciate hearing from you.

7 Gypsies
(877) 749-7797
www.sevengypsies.com

A2Z Essentials
(419) 663-2869
www.geta2z.com

Adobe Systems Incorporated
(800) 833-6687
www.adobe.com

Adorn It / Carolee's Creations
(435) 563-1100
www.adornit.com

American Crafts
(801) 226-0747
www.americancrafts.com

American Traditional Designs
(800) 448-6656
www.americantraditional.com

Anna Griffin, Inc.
(888) 817-8170
www.annagriffin.com

ANW Crestwood
(973) 406-5000
www.anwcrestwood.com

Arctic Frog
(479) 636-3764
www.arcticfrog.com

Around The Block
(801) 593-1946
www.aroundtheblockproducts.com

Autumn Leaves
(800) 588-6707
www.autumnleaves.com

Avery Dennison Corporation
(800) 462-8379
www.avery.com

BasicGrey
(801) 544-1116
www.basicgrey.com

Bazzill Basics Paper
(480) 558-8557
www.bazzillbasics.com

Berwick Offray, LLC
(800) 344-5533
www.offray.com

Bitstream
(800) 522-3668
www.bitstream.com

Blue Sky Designs
(662) 890-7380
www.blue-skydesigns.com

Board Dudes, Inc.
(951) 808-9347
www.boarddudes.com

Bobarbo
(418) 748-6775
www.bobarbo.com

Bo-Bunny Press
(801) 771-4010
www.bobunny.com

Buttons Galore & More
(856) 753-6700
www.buttonsgaloreandmore.com

CARL Mfg. USA, Inc.
(800) 257-4771
www.Carl-Products.com

Chatterbox, Inc.
(888) 416-6260
www.chatterboxinc.com

CherryArte
(212) 465-3495
www.cherryarte.com

Close To My Heart
(888) 655-6552
www.closetomyheart.com

Club Scrap, Inc.
(888) 634-9100
www.clubscrap.com

Colorbök, Inc.
(800) 366-4660
www.colorbok.com

Craf-T Products
www.craf-tproducts.com

Crafts, Etc. Ltd.
(800) 888-0321 x 1275
www.craftsetc.com

Crate Paper
(702) 966-0409
www.cratepaper.com

Creating Keepsakes
(888) 247-5282
www.creatingkeepsakes.com

Creative Imaginations
(800) 942-6487
www.cigift.com

Creative Memories
(800) 468-9335
www.creativememories.com

Dafont
www.dafont.com

Daisy D's Paper Company
(888) 601-8955
www.daisydspaper.com

Darice, Inc.
(800) 321-1494
www.darice.com

DDDesigns7
www.dddesigns7.com

Déjà Views
(800) 243-8419
www.dejaviews.com

Delta Technical Coatings, Inc.
(800) 423-4135
www.deltacrafts.com

Deluxe Designs
(480) 497-9005
www.deluxecuts.com

Designer Digitals
www.designerdigitals.com

Destination Scrapbook Designs
(866) 806-7826
www.destinationstickers.com

Die Cuts With A View
(801) 224-6766
www.diecutswithaview.com

Digi Chick, The
www.thedigichick.com

Digital Design Essentials
www.digitaldesignessentials.com

DMC Corp.
(973) 589-0606
www.dmc-usa.com

Doodlebug Design Inc.
(877) 800-9190
www.doodlebug.ws

Dream Street Papers
(480) 275-9736
www.dreamstreetpapers.com

Dymo
(800) 426-7827
www.dymo.com

Educational Insights
(800) 995-4436
www.edin.com

EK Success, Ltd.
(800) 524-1349
www.eksuccess.com

Everlasting Keepsakes by faith
(816) 896-7037
www.everlastingkeepsakes.com

Fancy Pants Designs, LLC
(801) 779-3212
www.fancypantsdesigns.com

Fiskars, Inc.
(866) 348-5661
www.fiskars.com

Flair Designs
(888) 546-9990
www.flairdesignsinc.com

Fontwerks
(604) 942-3105
www.fontwerks.com

Gel•a•tins
(800) 393-2151
www.gelatinstamps.com

Heidi Grace Designs, Inc.
(866) 348-5661
www.heidigrace.com

Heidi Swapp/Advantus Corporation
(904) 482-0092
www.heidiswapp.com

Hero Arts Rubber Stamps, Inc.
(800) 822-4376
www.heroarts.com

Hillcreek Designs
(619) 562-5799
www.hillcreekdesigns.com

Hobby Lobby Stores, Inc.
www.hobbylobby.com

Hot Off The Press
(888) 300-3406
www.paperwishes.com

Imagination Project, Inc.
(888) 477-6532
www.imaginationproject.com

Impress Rubber Stamps
(206) 901-9101
www.impressrubberstamps.com

In a Blink of an Eye
(877) 864-4781
www.inablinkofaneye.com

Inspire Graphics
www.creativedelights.com

Jen Wilson Designs
www.jenwilsondesigns.com

Jenni Bowlin
www.jennibowlin.com

Jo-Ann Stores
www.joann.com

Junkitz
(732) 792-1108
www.junkitz.com

K & Company
(888) 244-2083
www.kandcompany.com

Karen Foster Design
(801) 451-9779
www.karenfosterdesign.com

Karen Russell
www.karenrussell.typepad.com

KI Memories
(972) 243-5595
www.kimemories.com

Krylon
(800) 457-9566
www.krylon.com

Laura Ashley Papers -
no longer available

Legacy Paper Arts
www.legacypaperarts.com

Li'l Davis Designs
(480) 223-0080
www.lildavisdesigns.com

Magic Mesh
(651) 345-6374
www.magicmesh.com

Magic Scraps
(904) 482-0092
www.magicscraps.com

Magistical Memories
(818) 842-1540
www.magisticalmemories.com

Magnetic Poetry
(800) 370-7697
www.magneticpoetry.com

Making Memories
(801) 294-0430
www.makingmemories.com

Mara-Mi, Inc.
(800) 627-2648
www.mara-mi.com

Match'em Ups
(877) 300-0079
www.matchemups.com

Maya Road, LLC
(214) 488-3279
www.mayaroad.com

May Arts
(800) 442-3950
www.mayarts.com

me & my BiG ideas
(949) 583-2065
www.meandmybigideas.com

Melissa Frances /
Heart & Home, Inc.
(888) 616-6166
www.melissafrances.com

Memories Complete, LLC
(866) 966-6365
www.memoriescomplete.com

Michaels Arts & Crafts
(800) 642-4235
www.michaels.com

Microsoft Corporation
www.microsoft.com

Miss Elizabeth's
no source available

Mrs. Grossman's Paper Company
(800) 429-4549
www.mrsgrossmans.com

Mustard Moon
(763) 493-5157
www.mustardmoon.com

My Mind's Eye, Inc.
(866) 989-0320
www.mymindseye.com

Nunn Design
(800) 761-3557
www.nunndesign.com

Offray
see Berwick Offray, LLC

Paper Company, The
see ANW Crestwood

Paper Loft, The
(801) 254-1961
www.paperloft.com

Paper Salon
(800) 627-2648
www.papersalon.com

Paper Studio
(480) 557-5700
www.paperstudio.com

Pebbles Inc.
(801) 235-1520
www.pebblesinc.com

Petaloo
(800) 458-0350
www.petaloo.com

Plaid Enterprises, Inc.
(800) 842-4197
www.plaidonline.com

Pressed Petals
(800) 748-4656
www.pressedpetals.com

Prima Marketing, Inc.
(909) 627-5532
www.primamarketinginc.com

Provo Craft
(800) 937-7686
www.provocraft.com

PSX Design
www.sierra-enterprises.com/psx-main

Queen & Co.
(858) 613-7858
www.queenandcompany.com

Ranger Industries, Inc.
(800) 244-2211
www.rangerink.com

Royal & Langnickel /
Royal Brush Mfg.
(800) 247-2211
www.royalbrush.com

Rusty Pickle
(801) 746-1045
www.rustypickle.com

Sakura Hobby Craft
(310) 212-7878
www.sakuracraft.com

Sandylion Sticker Designs
(800) 387-4215
www.sandylion.com

Sassafras Lass
(801) 269-1331
www.sassafraslass.com

Scenic Route Paper Co.
(801) 225-5754
www.scenicroutepaper.com

Scissor Sisters
(877) 773-7786
www.scissor-sisters.com

Scrapsupply
(615) 777-3953
www.scrapsupply.com

Scrapbook Graphics
www.scrapbookgraphics.com

ScrapVillage
www.scrapvillage.com

Scrapworks, LLC /
As You Wish Products, LLC
(801) 363-1010
www.scrapworks.com

SEI, Inc.
(800) 333-3279
www.shopsei.com

Shabby Princess
www.shabbyprincess.com

Sizzix
(877) 355-4766
www.sizzix.com

Sonburn, Inc.
(800) 436-4919
www.sonburn.com

Stampin' Up!
(800) 782-6787
www.stampinup.com

Sticker Studio
(888) 244-2083
www.stickerstudio.com

Sweetwater
(800) 359-3094
www.sweetwaterscrapbook.com

Target
www.target.com

Therm O Web, Inc.
(800) 323-0799
www.thermoweb.com

Three Bugs in a Rug, LLC
(801) 804-6657
www.threebugsinarug.com

Two Peas in a Bucket
(888) 896-7327
www.twopeasinabucket.com

Urban Lily
www.urbanlily.com

USArtQuest, Inc.
(517) 522-6225
www.usartquest.com

Wal-Mart Stores, Inc.
www.walmart.com

Waste Not Paper
(800) 867-2737
www.wastenotpaper.com

We R Memory Keepers, Inc.
(801) 539-5000
www.weronthenet.com

Westrim Crafts
(800) 727-2727
www.westrimcrafts.com

WorldWin Papers
(888) 834-6455
www.worldwinpapers.com

index